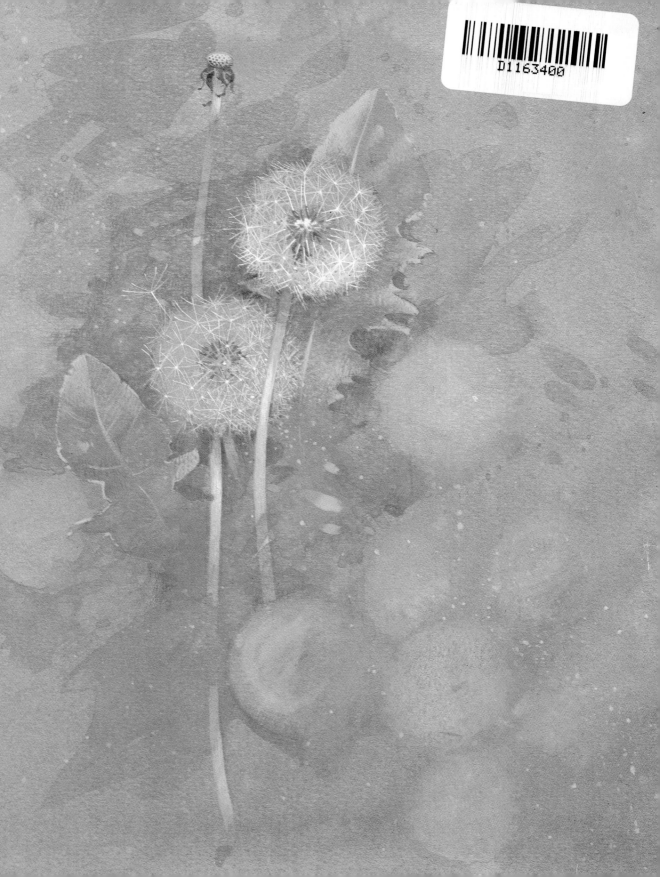

Beningfield's Countryside

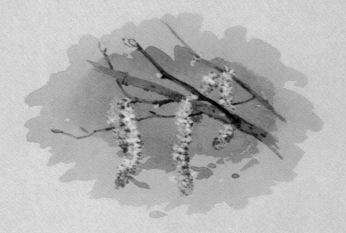

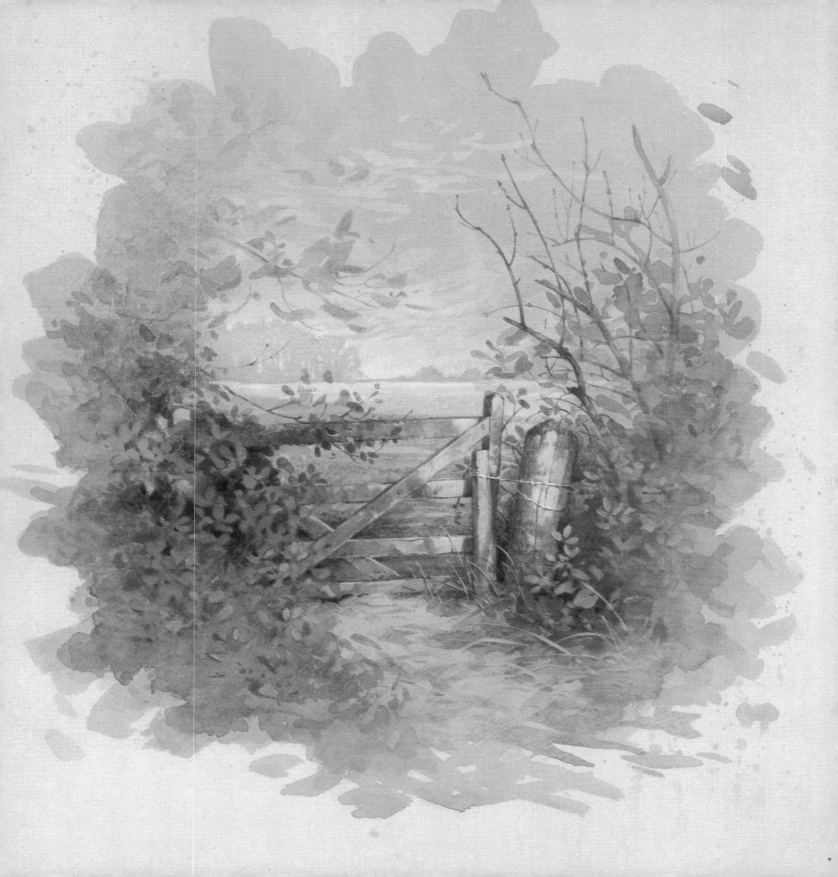

Beningfield's Countryside

GORDON BENINGFIELD

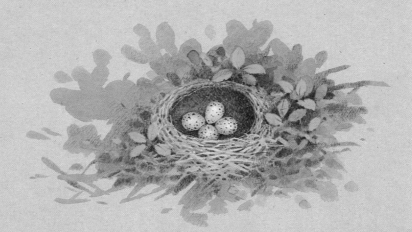

A Studio Book
THE VIKING PRESS
New York

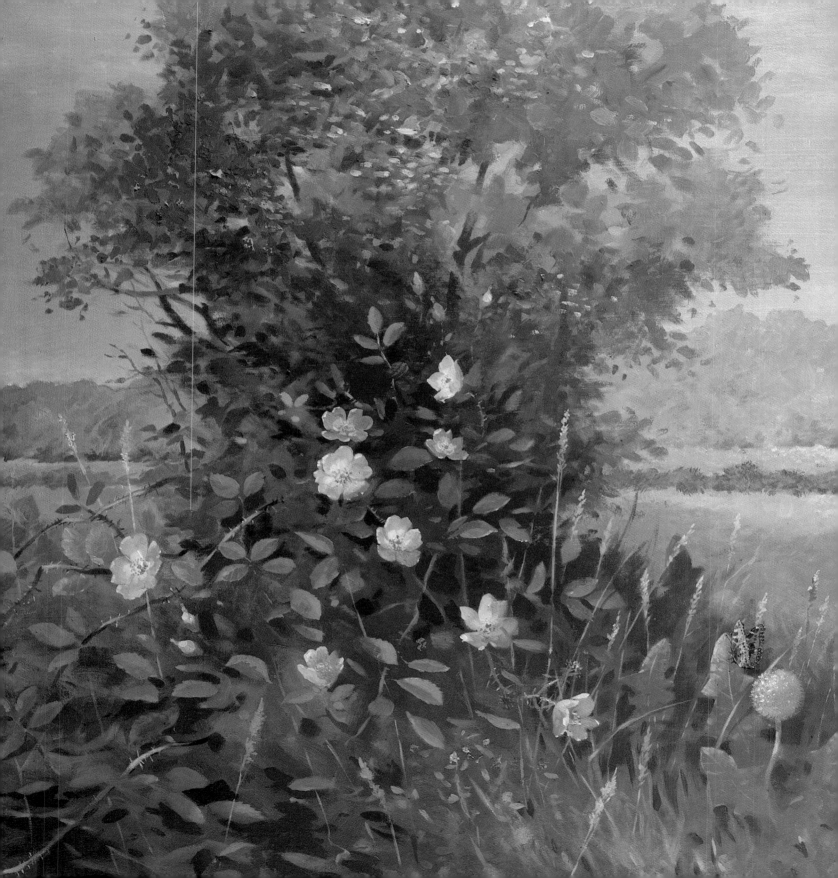

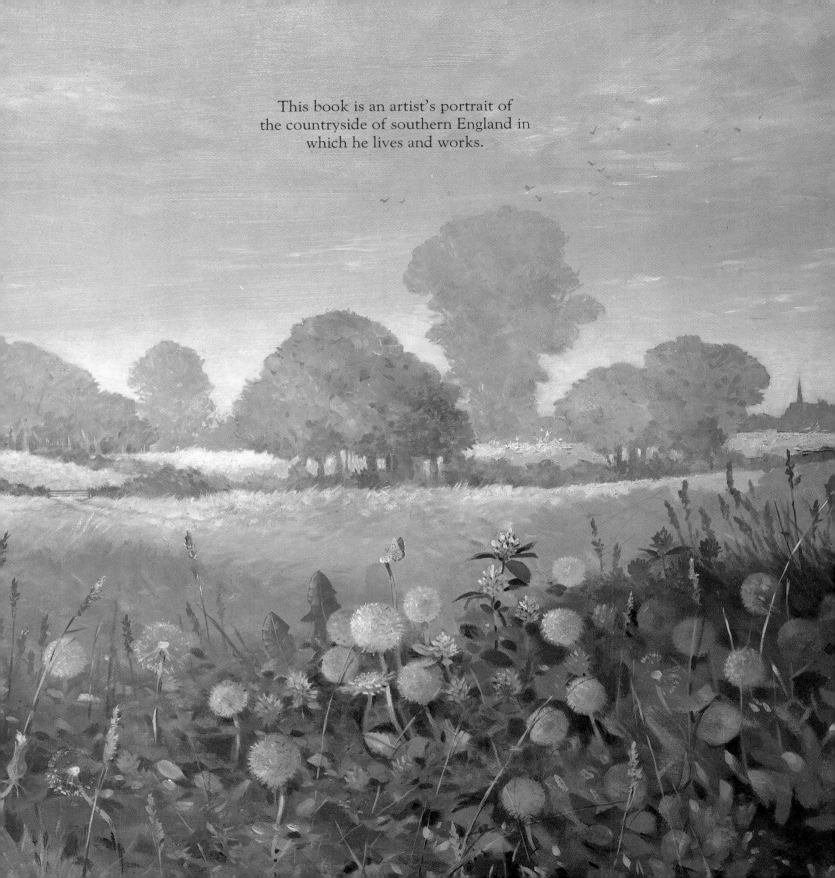

This book is an artist's portrait of
the countryside of southern England in
which he lives and works.

Copyright © Gordon Beningfield (pictures)
and Cameron & Tayleur Books Ltd, 1980

First published in 1980 by The Viking Press
625 Madison Avenue, New York, N.Y. 10022

Published simultaneously in Canada by
Penguin Books Canada Limited

Library of Congress Cataloging in Publication Data
Beningfield, Gordon, 1936–
Beningfield's Countryside.

(A Studio Book)
1. Natural History – England. 2. Man – Influence
on nature – England. I. Title. II. Title:
Countryside.
QH138.A1 B46   1980   574.942   80–5366
ISBN 0-670-15815-1

Edited and designed by Ian Cameron
Produced by Cameron & Tayleur (Books) Limited
25 Lloyd Baker Street, London WC1
Printed in Holland

Contents

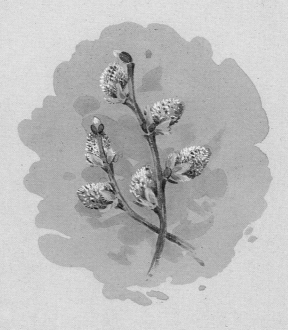

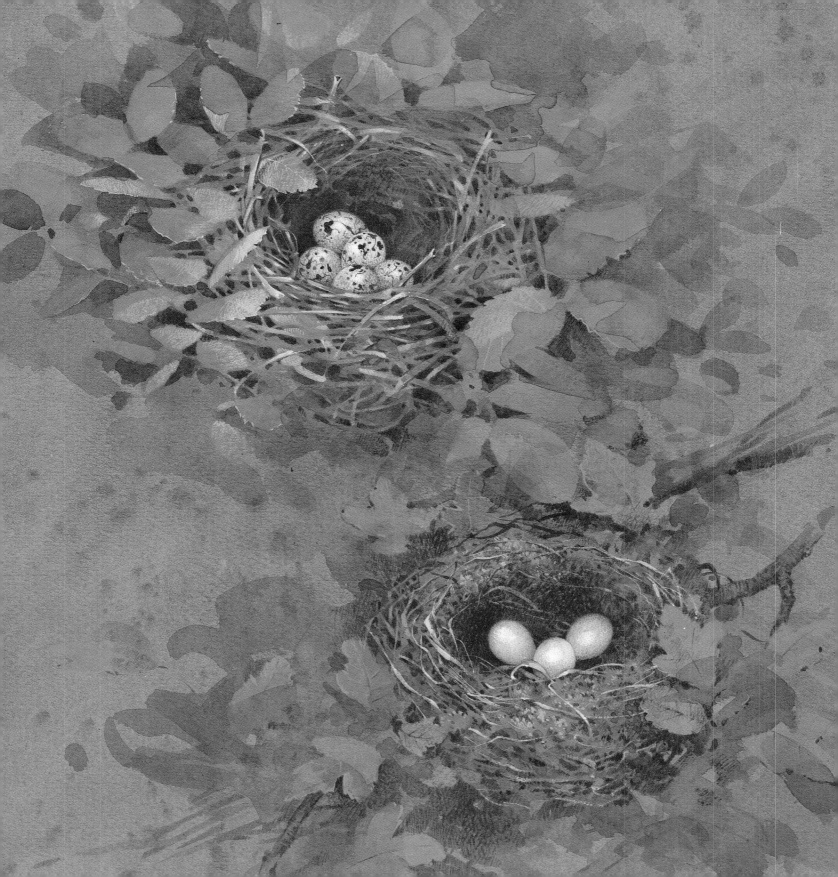

Introduction

If it had not been for the war, I would probably have been brought up in London, where my father worked on the River Thames. I was only three when my family moved to Hertfordshire, ten miles or so from my present home, and I have lived in the area ever since. Living in London would not have stopped me being an artist, but without my early immersion in the countryside, I might well have found other subject matter.

At the village school, any of us who wanted were allowed two weeks a year off to do farm work. I always seized the opportunity and went picking fruit or potatoes – any sort of schoolboy casual labour. Each year, I managed to forget that I had to go back after a fortnight and stayed on the

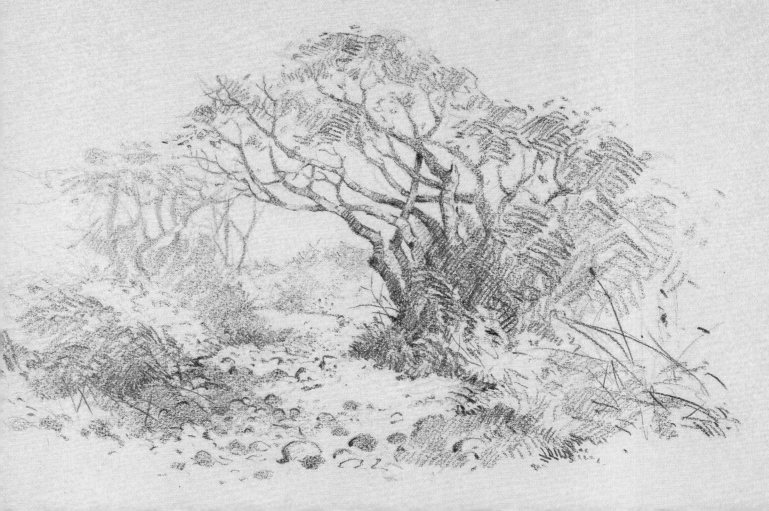

farm for a couple of weeks after the other boys had returned. Luckily, my headmaster, who obviously had a good idea of what my future might be, seemed to feel that the extra weeks' working on the land could only help me. He never hauled me back to school. His attitude to my painting was much the same: he would let me paint for days on end, when all the other pupils were doing the academic subjects that I found rather boring and difficult.

Even at that early stage, I saw myself becoming a painter. I had the advantage that my father was an enthusiastic amateur artist and was able to give me more than encouragement; he helped me to learn about technique to an extent that surprised my art master at school. During the war, he used to take me on the crossbar of his bicycle round the country lanes when he went to sketch and paint. At six or seven years old, I used to sit and draw with my father.

In those days, I mainly drew birds and mammals, creatures like mice and small deer. It was the time when the big film for children was *Bambi*. Terrifying and upsetting though it sometimes was, it had me drawing fawns and wise old owls, copies of the Walt Disney animals, which I also used to model in plasticine. In the countryside I saw mainly the commonplace creatures like rooks and partridges and the abundance of rabbits that you could expect to see scampering around on any country lane. To begin with, though, it was easier for me, as for any other child, not to draw reality but to work from someone else's interpretation of it, and *Bambi* was the most powerful interpretation I knew.

However, I did attempt to draw some of the things that I saw in the country, and I also tried my hand at landscapes because my father was quite keen on painting them. Right from the start, my work revolved around animal life rather than humans – people have very rarely attracted me as subjects. Perhaps it was because the country was the background to my growing up that I never became obsessed with any particular aspect of it; my fascination was with the countryside in general – I just loved being there.

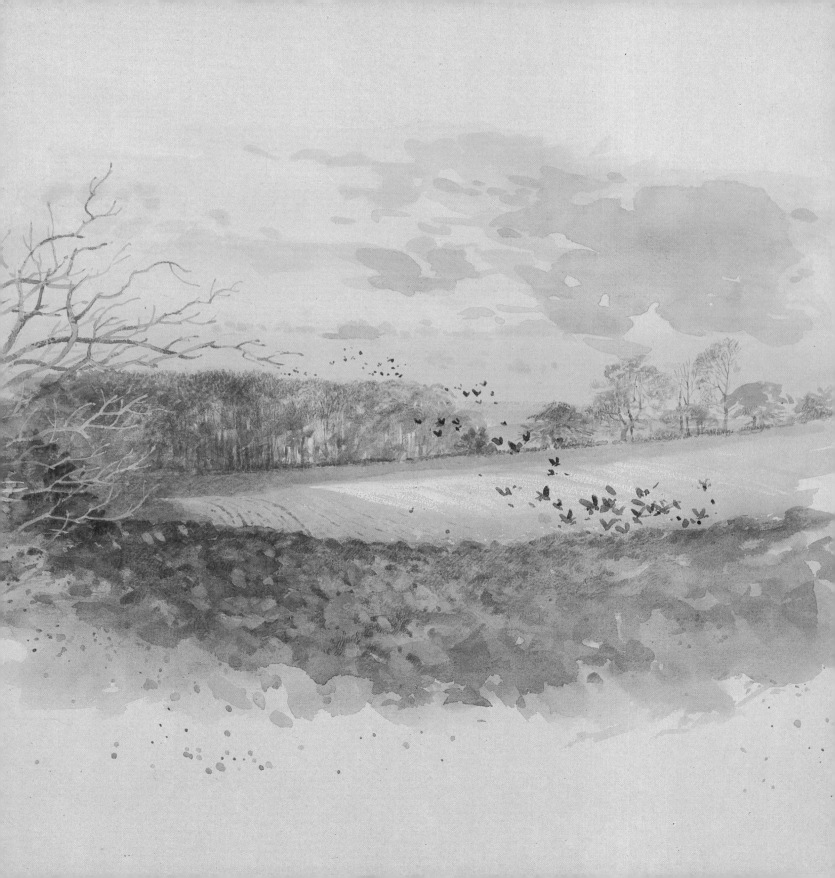

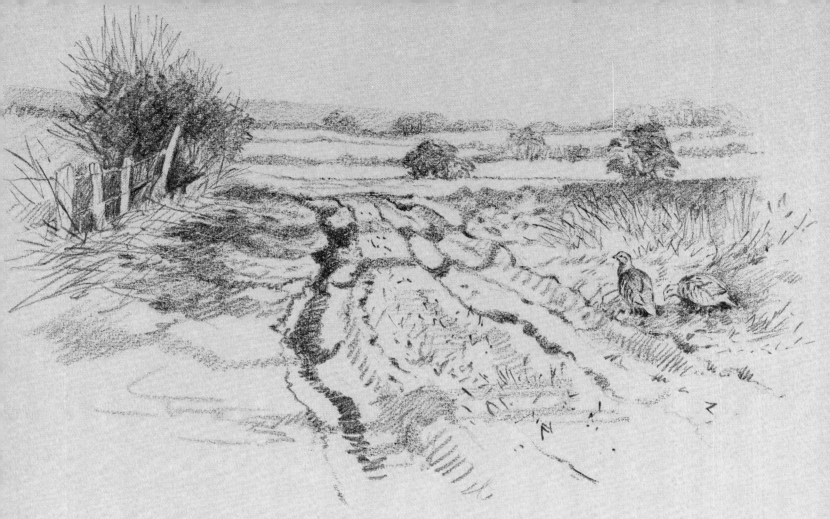

You must remember that in those days – during and just after the war – the countryside was a very much richer place than it is today. The hedge-rows that separated the small, lush meadows were big and dense, with massive hawthorns and often quite large groups of trees. Farming then was on a much smaller scale and mainly mixed; most of the farms had cattle and did a bit of general crop-growing. They all had chickens running around the yards, and free-range pigs.

I would go out with the other boys from the village, rambling around the fields as country children do. We looked at birds and tried to catch frogs and newts – most meadows seemed to have a suitable pond. At harvest time, we would follow the binder around to see the great wealth of wildlife that leapt out of the shrinking area of the uncut crop: above all, rabbits and mice, but also a few hares and often a fox; among the birds, there would be partridges and even an occasional corncrake. In September and October, the stubble fields would burst with coveys of partridges as you walked across them.

Without the vast and noisy machinery that is now on the land, the countryside was very much quieter. We used to play games in the lane; it was the only flat area where we could play hopscotch or roller-skate (on one skate – we couldn't afford two). Once in a while, there would be a grumbling noise in the distance which would be a pre-war car. There was plenty of time to step out of the way, and it might be an hour before another one appeared. The quiet, lush countryside of only thirty years ago was a very different world from the one we know today, but it is the world that lies behind all my paintings.

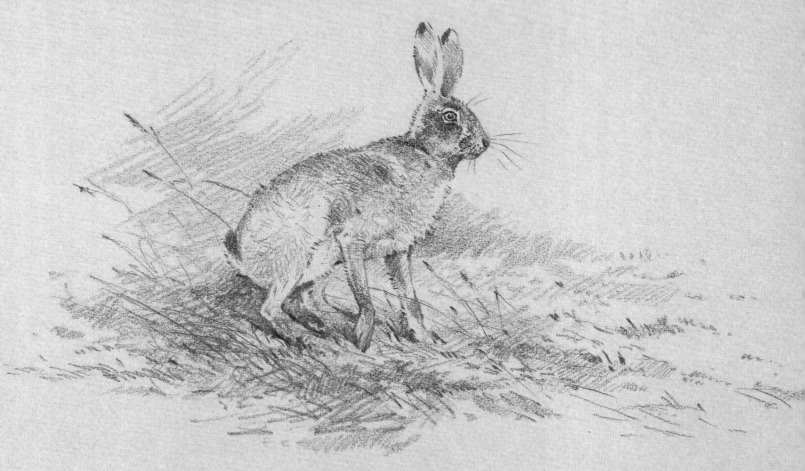

Now that so many hedgerows have gone and meadows have been ploughed up, the landscape is open and airy. It has lost the intimate and enclosed quality that I liked so much. Nevertheless there are still pockets that have been left as they were, particularly in Dorset, which has changed far less than most counties in southern England. The deep combes will, with luck, always be difficult to farm, and because they are quite unsuitable for large-scale cereal growing, there has been no reason to uproot the deep, thick hedgerows. I go to Dorset to find the sort of country where there are always corners to turn and gateways that you want to go through to look for the hidden excitements that lie beyond. But thanks to the big estates, some of this quality, which for me is the essence of rural England, still survives in Hertfordshire.

This is the environment in which I am most happy; I am sure that I would have gone to work on the land when I left school if I had not had the opportunity to be an ecclesiastical artist and to go to art school. For about ten years, I was very much involved with matters of technique and with my new profession. Even then, if I was working in a country church, I would go out into the churchyard and paint or draw. If it was a town church, I tended to stay inside.

When I was in my fairly early twenties, after I got married, my natural instincts took me back to the countryside. I still think that if I had not become an artist, I would have been a farm worker or a gamekeeper. I might even have gone to the great length of becoming a shepherd. I roamed around at weekends with my dog, and I started fishing and looking at birds and butterflies again. With my wife's encouragement, I returned, purely for pleasure, to painting what I saw, just as I had done years back, but now with the craftsmanship that I had learned through my ecclesiastical work. The first pictures simply involved the things we did at the weekends, but before long I had entirely transformed my subject matter. Since then I have devoted myself completely to painting the English countryside.

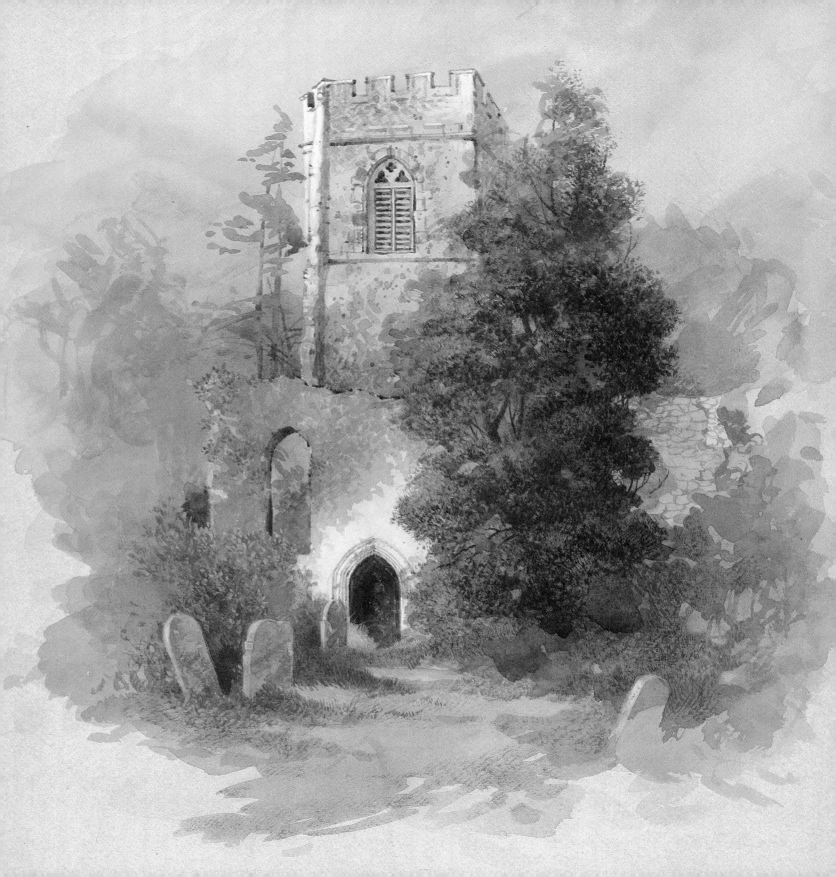

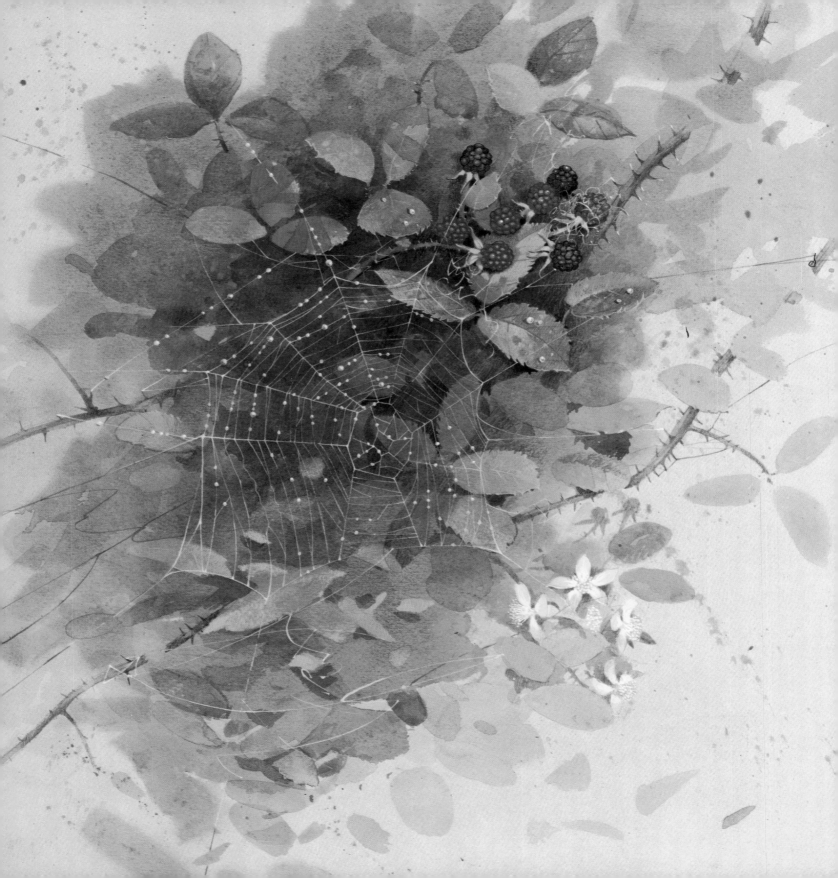

My work is quite the opposite of scientific book illustration, which sets out to display a particular animal or plant in a way that shows exactly what it looks like and what the points of recognition are. I want to capture seasons and moods to such an extent that you can almost smell the subject of the picture, whether it is a portrait of a fox or a landscape of a bluebell wood. I cannot paint even a single animal without being strongly aware of its surroundings and the way it fits into them. Above all, then, I try to communicate this awareness so that anyone who sees the picture cannot help but feel how the animal belongs in its environment. My main theme is not just wildlife but the countryside as a whole.

Because I set out in my painting to celebrate the aspects of the country that I love, I cannot help being constantly aware of the destruction of rural England going on all around me. I remember great quantities of spiders' webs draped and laced along the hedgerows in autumn. You can still see them, but now there seem to be far fewer webs and, worse still, far fewer hedgerows. Grasshoppers and crickets used to set up a huge racket at twilight, but today you would have to go to out-of-the-way places like the unspoilt parts of Dorset to find them in any numbers. I used to enjoy watching sparrowhawks hunting across the hedgerows, but you would now be very lucky to catch as much as a glimpse of one in Hertfordshire. There has been a drastic depletion of both the quantity and the variety of wildlife.

Drenching the land with chemicals and taking away the established habitats have both severely upset the balance of nature. Perhaps only wood pigeons have been unaffected by the use of chemicals. They descend in hordes on the big cereal fields and do terrible things to the brussels sprouts in the market gardens of Bedfordshire. Still, I would hate to see them drastically reduced in numbers. The sound of a wood pigeon echoing through the woods in early summer is something that is very important to me. As to the damage they undoubtedly do, I am sure that this is something we must accept. The way to have no damage would be to have no wildlife.

Inevitably some species have suffered more than others. The kestrel is doing very well, but the sparrowhawk suffered badly because the small birds that it fed on had taken in the chemical sprays with their food. Now, at last, it is beginning very slowly to recover. Again, magpies have become more plentiful, but there are certainly not as many rooks as there used to be in rookeries like the one in front of my cottage.

Among the wildlife that I particularly miss is the partridge, which used to be one of the most common birds on arable land but now has become very scarce in southern England. For me, another sad loss is newts. Once, every pond seemed to have a newt in it. I can well remember the excitement of finding newts and seeing their yellow spotted bellies. Not many present-day children are likely to have the thrill of going newting.

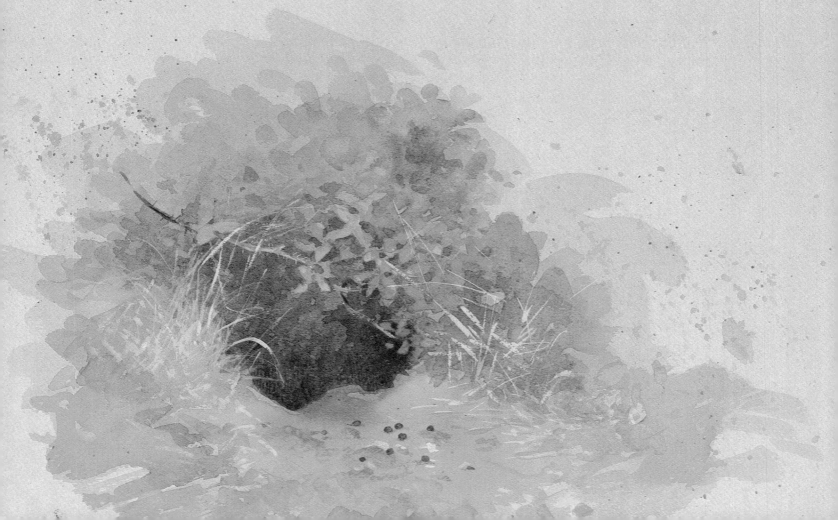

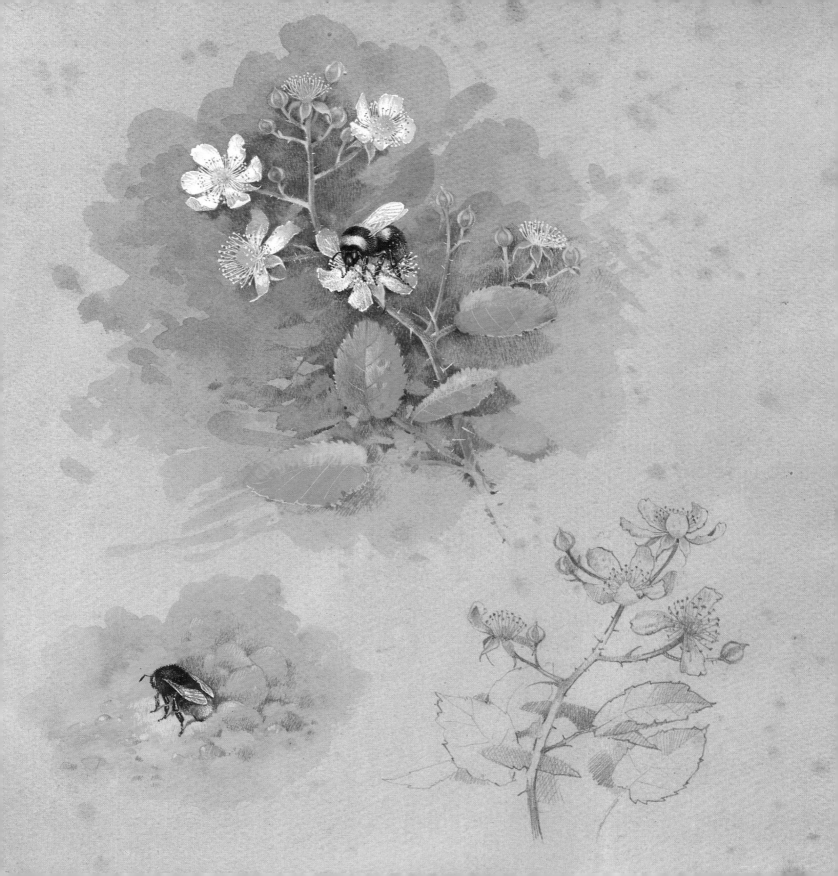

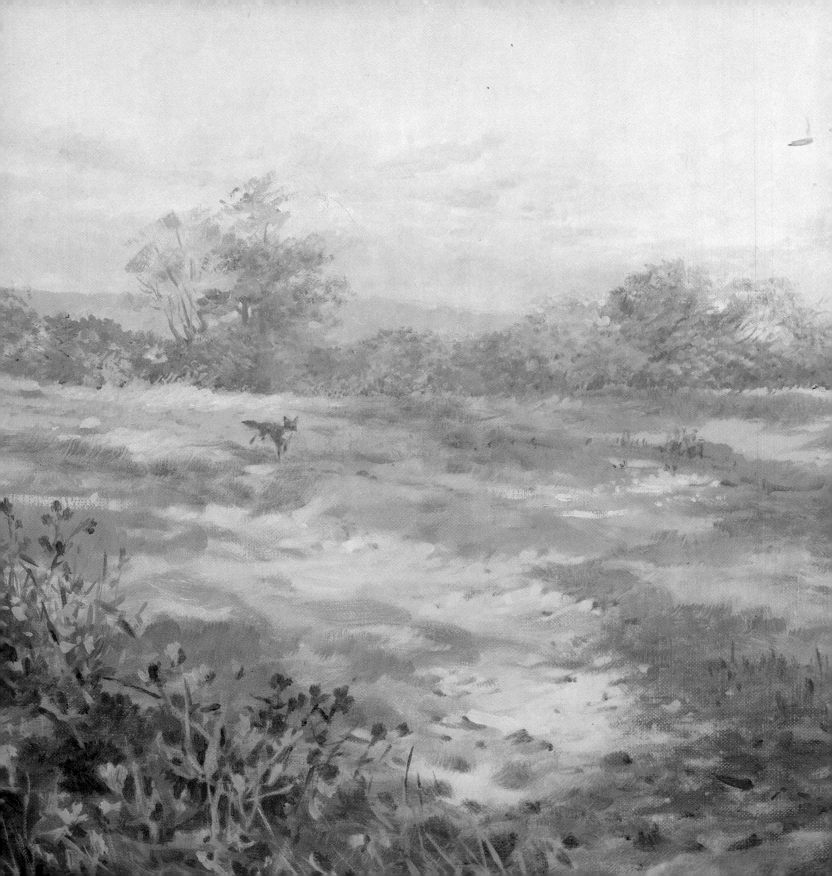

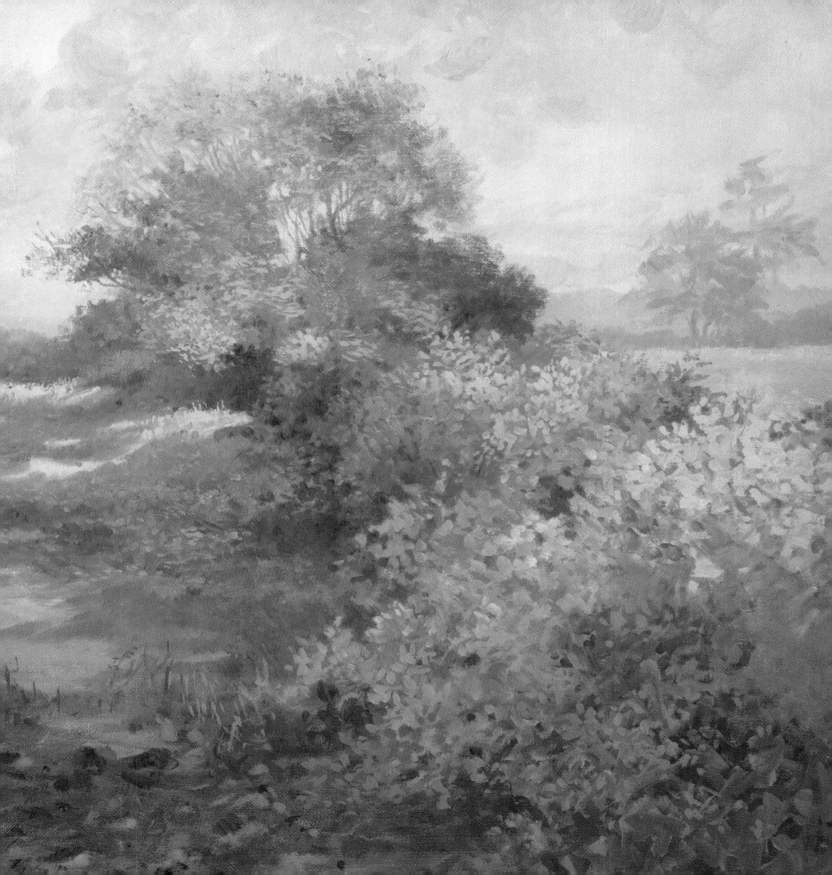

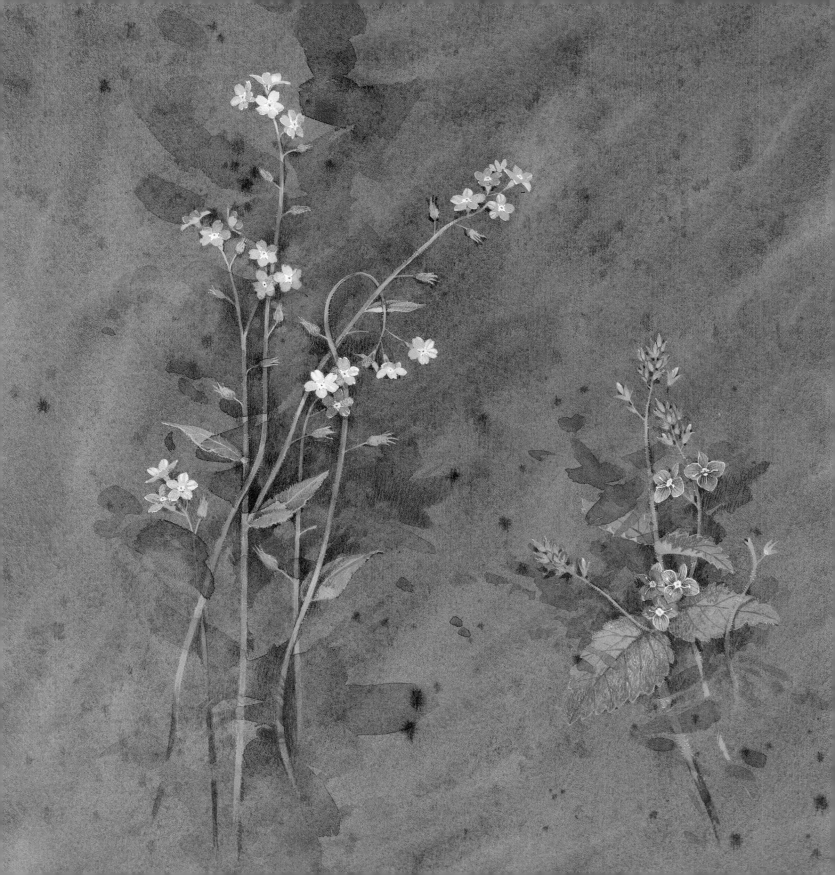

What has happened to the countryside is that it has been tidied up and rationalized in the interests of productivity. Of course, by clearing out the unremunerative areas, we are taking away the habitats of our wildlife. We cannot do that and expect the wildlife still to be there. For the animals, the tidying of the countryside has the same sort of impact there would be on us if all our houses were knocked down and all the shops were taken away so that we could not get any food.

As an artist, I can see no visual attraction in vast areas of prairie corn with hardly a tree and certainly not a hedgerow left. What is more, this landscape is completely divorced from the traditions of the British countryside, and it is getting worse all the time. Each autumn, there is the further devastation of straw and stubble burning on a large scale – any trees that happen to be left are likely to be so heavily scorched that they will be dead within two or three years. The irony is that in the days of the horse-drawn plough, the land was, I believe, giving a greater yield per acre than it does today. Many more people were needed to work it – apparently the modern idea of efficiency in agriculture, as in industry, is to use technology instead of people.

The cereal prairies lack any of the incidental attractions that used to be found in cornfields. If there are extraneous plants like poppies and cornflowers, it is considered bad farming. Even at the edges of the fields, the spraying and clearing out has removed the flora and fauna that always went with arable land. Twenty years ago, the situation was perhaps even worse: I remember going in the early 'sixties to see the gamekeeper on an estate near my home. I found him sitting in his game larder with a pile four feet high of dead mammals and birds. Here was an estate that was spending considerable sums of money rearing game birds and more money still on chemicals which killed them all off.

Even though agriculture has grown much more sophisticated in the past twenty years, the worries are still there. What control can there be over the strengths of the various chemicals that are used? In these matters, people are likely to work on a 'one for the pot' principle. It is impossible to know the full effect of what is happening, even to know exactly what is being squirted on the land. All manner of substances soak down to the water table and poison the trees, or drain from the land and pollute the rivers.

It would be much too easy to blame the fate of the countryside and its wildlife on the farmers, most of whom, I am sure, have their hearts in the right place. However, they have been encouraged in their activities, with government grants. We are all to blame, though, in demanding cheap food first and thinking about the environmental consequences second, if at all. Meanwhile the firms concerned have kept up a bombardment of leaflets filled with evidence to demonstrate the virtues of each new chemical, but with little to say about the effect on our wildlife. They do not say that once the farmer comes to rely heavily on chemicals to nourish his crops and kill the pests, he will be driven to become even more reliant on chemicals as the humus is lost from the soil and the natural predators are poisoned.

Life has changed so much that we forget what we used to see. I hope that sooner or later people of my generation will start thinking about the things they liked in the countryside when they were young – the things they like when they buy my pictures. Then perhaps the farmers will ask themselves if it would make very much difference to their yield if we had these things today. The ideal would be if more of them could be persuaded to be conservationists – there is no reason why good farming and conservation should be incompatible.

The countryside of southern England has been shaped entirely by man, but over the centuries this process was limited by the means that were available – nature had to be taken into account and often imposed itself on man's efforts. Hedgerows and trees could grow up because there were not the implements that made it easy to remove them. With the arrival of the flail, the mechanical hedge-cutting equipment which hacks away indiscriminately, there are not many saplings in the hedgerows that will have the chance of growing into trees. With the machinery and the chemicals that

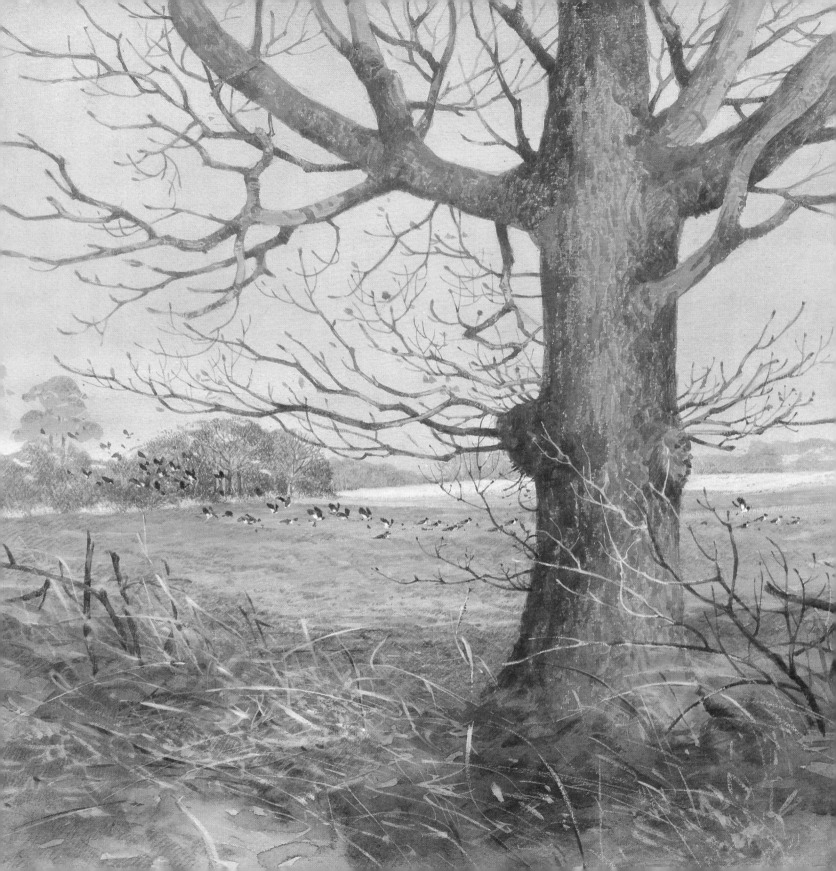

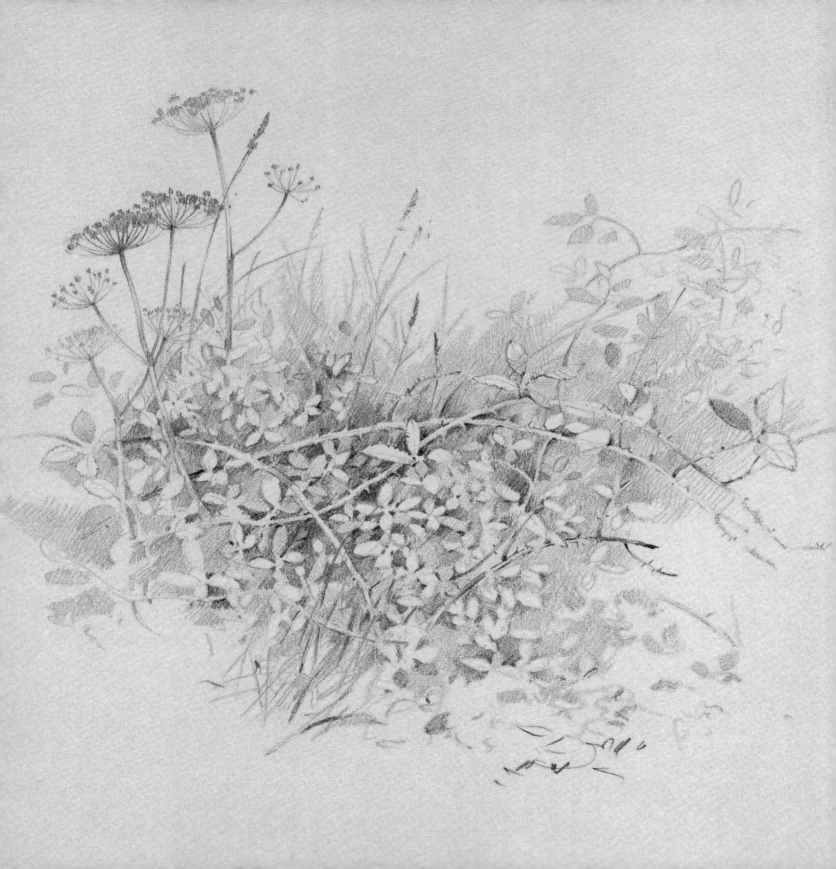

have been brought in since the war, human pressure has increased to the point where the countryside can no longer cope. It is crying out for help.

We are still just about at the stage when we can choose whether we want to save it. With nature's extraordinary facility for restoring itself, areas that are left alone for just a few years will regain a rich population of wildlife. Old railways lines are a case in point, as they make wonderful havens for butterflies. Conservation now is not just a matter of large blues and ospreys, although certainly the rarities must be protected at all costs. It is the ordinary things like small tortoiseshell butterflies and bluebell woods that are now disappearing and need to be protected. In fact, the urgent task for conservation is the countryside as a whole in all its variety and richness.

The pictures in this book chronicle some of the things I treasure in the English countryside. In many cases, they have been composed by bringing together elements I have observed at different times and places in order to evoke a particular environment or mood. Almost everything that has gone to make up the pictures, though, has been found either in Dorset or around my home in Hertfordshire. This book, then, is not intended as an exercise in nostalgia for what has been lost but as a celebration of the countryside that remains and can be preserved. I pray that it will have the same significance to future generations.

Gordon Beningfield

Water End
Hertfordshire

January 1980

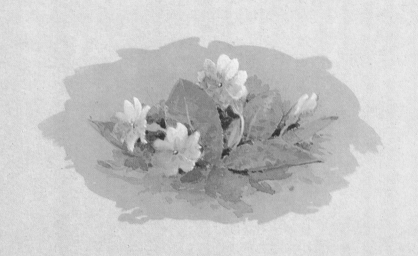

The Cottage

My cottage was built around 1600 and is rather unusual for its time in having quite high ceilings. In general, it is slightly larger than might be expected for a house of its kind. At some point, extra money must have been spent on it, as it has some quite elaborate old pine panelling. The dormer windows are certainly later additions, and there is a small extension at the back which must be at least two hundred years old.

We know very little of the history of the cottage – the records were largely lost when the big house went up in flames at the turn of the century. From an old map of the parish which names the various inhabitants, we know that in 1838 the cottage was occupied by a man called Zebediah Hooker and his wife, Virtue Hooker. For about a century before we arrived, it was the home of the Fowler family, who still live nearby in the old wheelwright's and corn merchant's house. The corn merchant's business was actually started in the cottage by Mr Fowler's father, who had previously worked at the mill lower down the river.

When we moved in, the building was very dilapidated, and the outside had black beams and white walls so that it looked like 1930s mock Tudor. Luckily, what had happened was more a cover-up job than a matter of destruction. It would have been very easy to bring in a builder and have the place modernized, but that would have produced an old modern house. I have been able to pick away, rather like an archaeologist, to find what is underneath. With the help of friends, I have uncovered beam ceilings and two inglenook fireplaces, which we were able very carefully to restore. Removing the lime wash from the outside walls was particularly hard work – it was virtually a matter of scraping down to the brick by hand. Now the timbers are a more natural colour and the brickwork is back to its proper light yellowish pink, you can see that many of the bricks are of the very early two-inch variety.

There was a small piece of the house missing when I bought it. Apparently, it had been in such bad condition that it had had to be demolished, but its outline was still traceable on the ground, and Mr Fowler produced a photograph from long before the war of his father standing outside, which showed what the missing part had been like. Because of the photograph, we were able to put it back exactly as it had been in the past. We did need builders to take off the cottage roof, but I asked them not to remove the moss when they took off the tiles. I was delighted to find that when the tiles were replaced, the moss was still intact. I suspect that the house was always tiled rather than thatched. Certainly the tiles are very old, with wooden pegs, and I imagine that they could be the original ones.

The cottage is on about an acre of ground which has never been soaked in chemicals or otherwise wrecked in any way. It is a fine piece of old countryside where violets and wild pansies flower and where February brings literally thousands of snowdrops. Apart from a small lawn at the front of the house and another at the back, the whole garden has been left to itself to become a haven for a wide variety of wildlife.

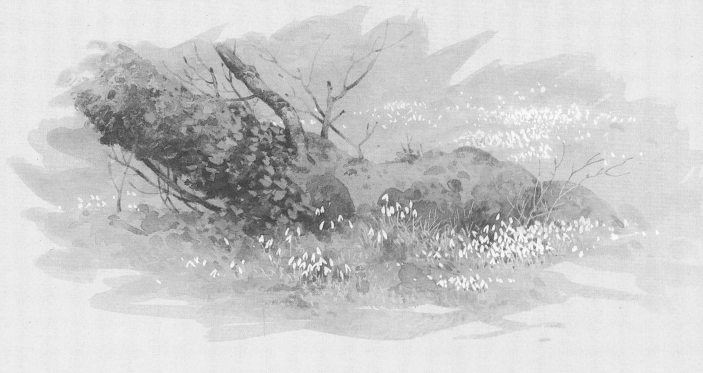

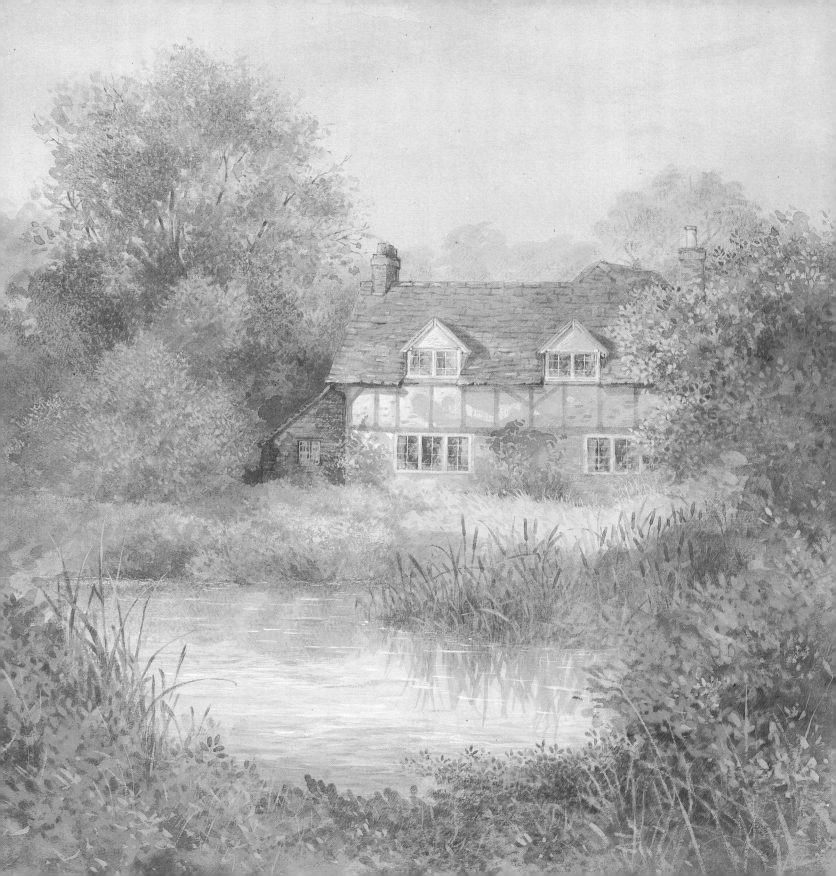

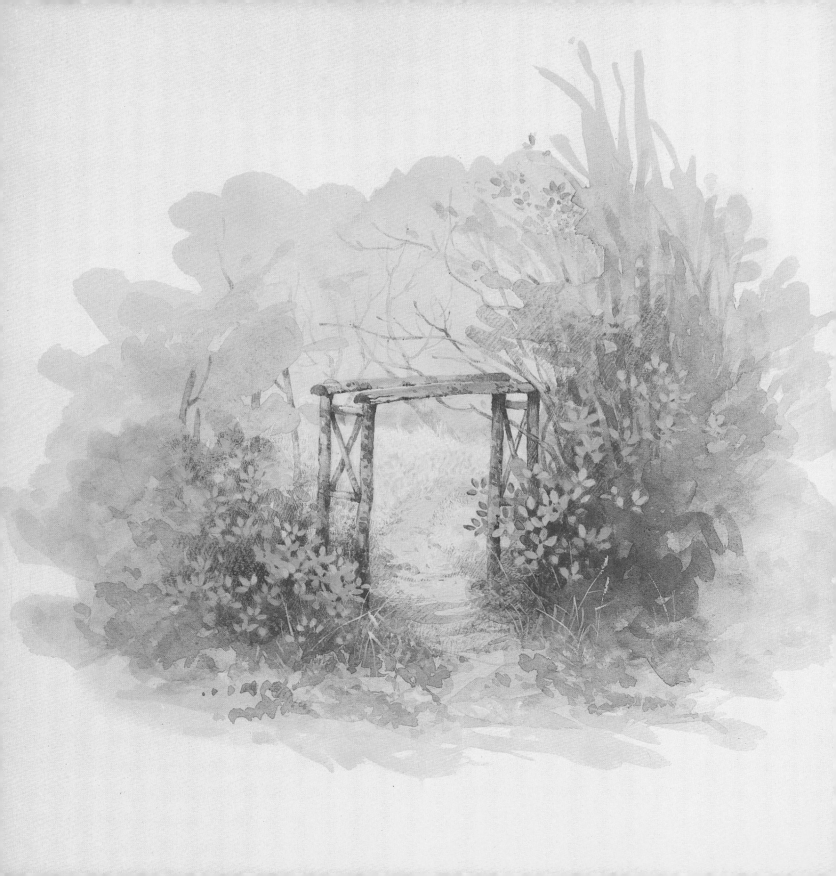

The things that I have planted are simple cottage-garden flowers which are not far removed from wild flowers – climbing roses, honesty, marigolds, lupins, hollyhocks and, of course, buddleia to attract the butterflies. I like flowers to smell sweet; most modern varieties lack scent in much the way that modern food lacks flavour. Honeysuckle and Victorian roses not only look attractive and true but smell nice as well. Apart from the simple flowers and about thirty trees that I have planted, everything else in the garden is wild. I do not share the attitude of many people who think that the best way to make a garden is to rip everything out and start from scratch – gardening seems to involve the same taste for destruction as agriculture and forestry. When I hear gardeners talking about weeds,

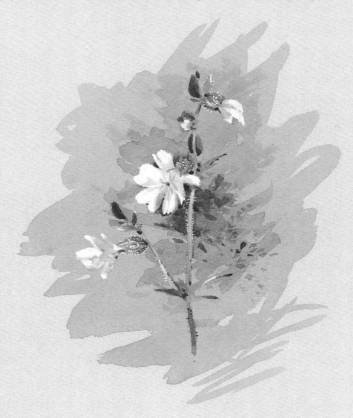

I wish they would call them wild flowers, which is, after all, what weeds really are. To my eye, most of the wild flowers that are unwelcome in well-kept gardens are more pleasing than the varieties that are planted.

Behind the cottage is a thick, old-fashioned hedge with hazel trees that I am told are unusually large. And behind the hedge is an old orchard with big apple trees covered in ivy, among which brimstone butterflies hibernate. I occasionally cut a small path in the dense undergrowth of the orchard so that I can walk though it, but otherwise the only thing I do to it is to cut the undergrowth back with a scythe each February to let in some air and light.

Most gardeners would think that my land was nothing more than a jungle, but even if I had something that was more like most people's idea

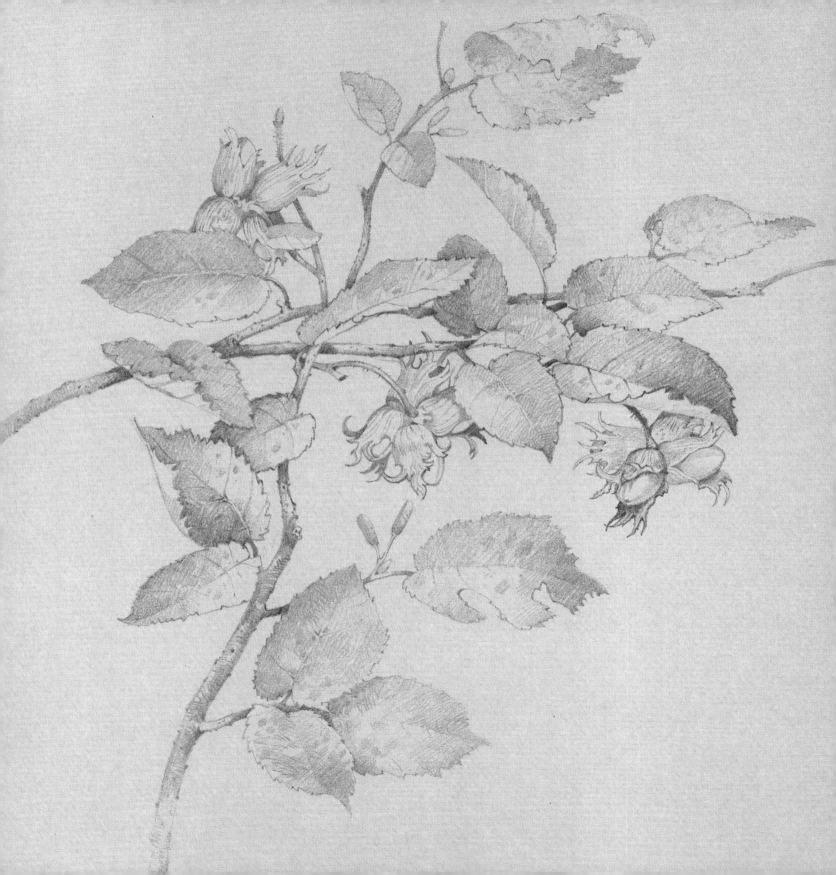

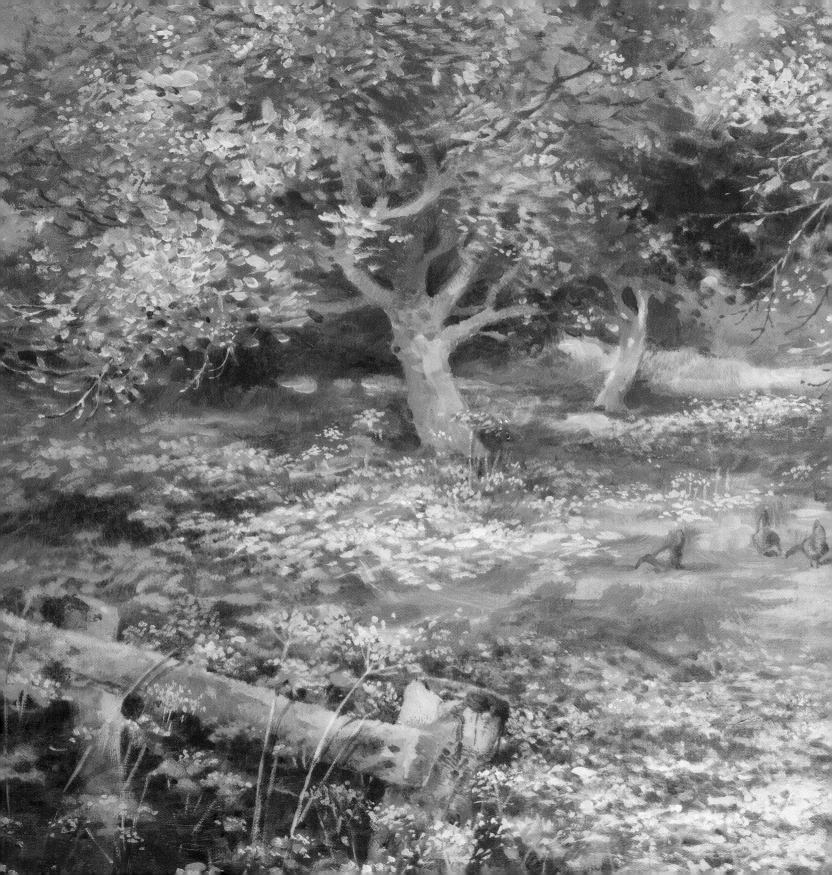

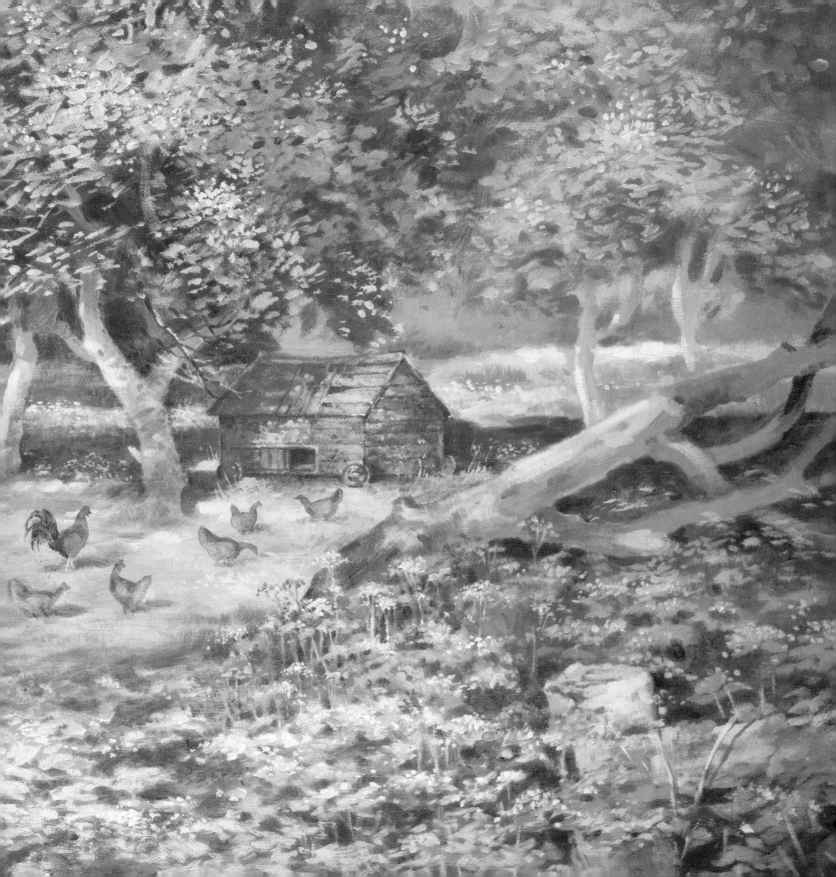

of a garden, I would still want it to be arranged so that I would not be able to see it all at once. For me, a garden has to be as full of secrets and surprises as the old, enclosed countryside. In mine, I have an inexhaustible mass of information for my pictures. If I need a background for a plant or animal study, I can go out there and find it. Such plants as hogweed, goatsbeard, thistles and bindweed have forms that constantly excite me, so that I want to return to them again and again.

It was my orchard in late spring that gave me the inspiration for my big orchard picture. There is a moment when the old apple trees are bursting with blossom and the cow parsley is also in flower. The whole place has a dappled, spotty texture, with the two kinds of blossom meeting and everything exploding with growth. The chickens in the picture are proper orchard chickens, just as they should be. In my own orchard I keep the gamecock that was given to me by Phil Drabble, who is an expert on these old fighting birds. The cock and the hen he gave me to go with it are now a very special part of my menagerie. I have set out in my picture of the gamecock to display it to the best possible advantage, rather in the manner of a nineteenth-century picture of a prize bird, but still to paint it as it actually is, without idealizing it.

In the summer months, when the orchard is a huge tangle of grass and hogweed, we have harvest mice nesting. They are also found in the reed

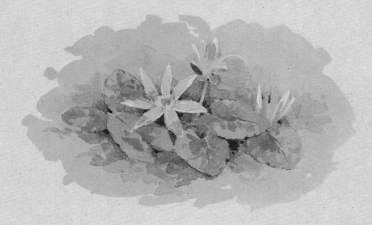

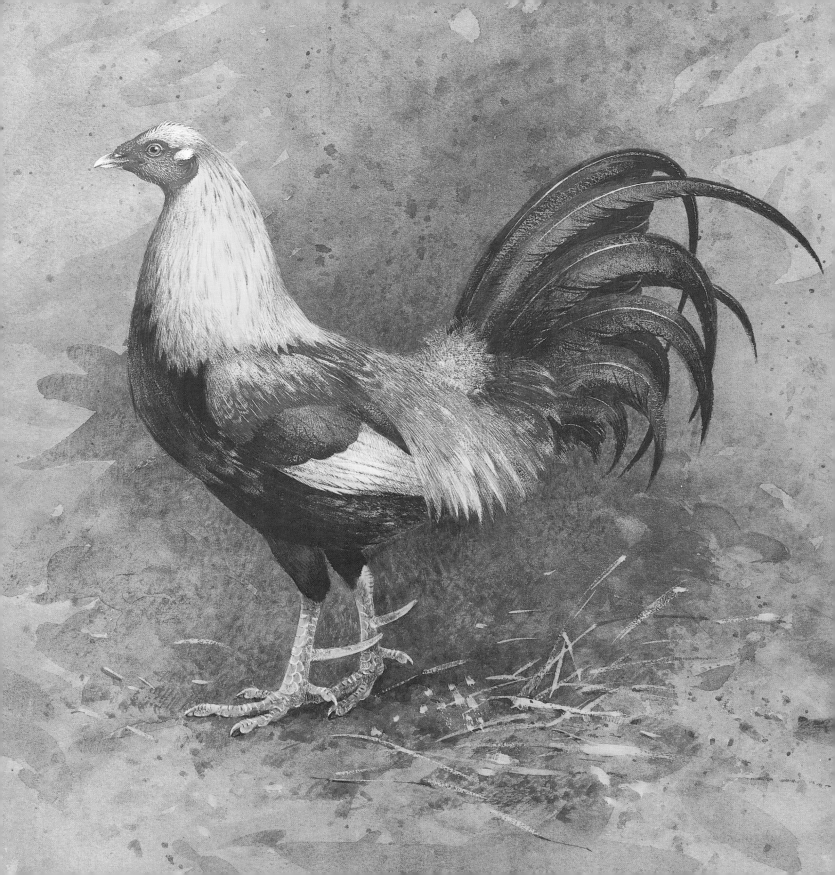

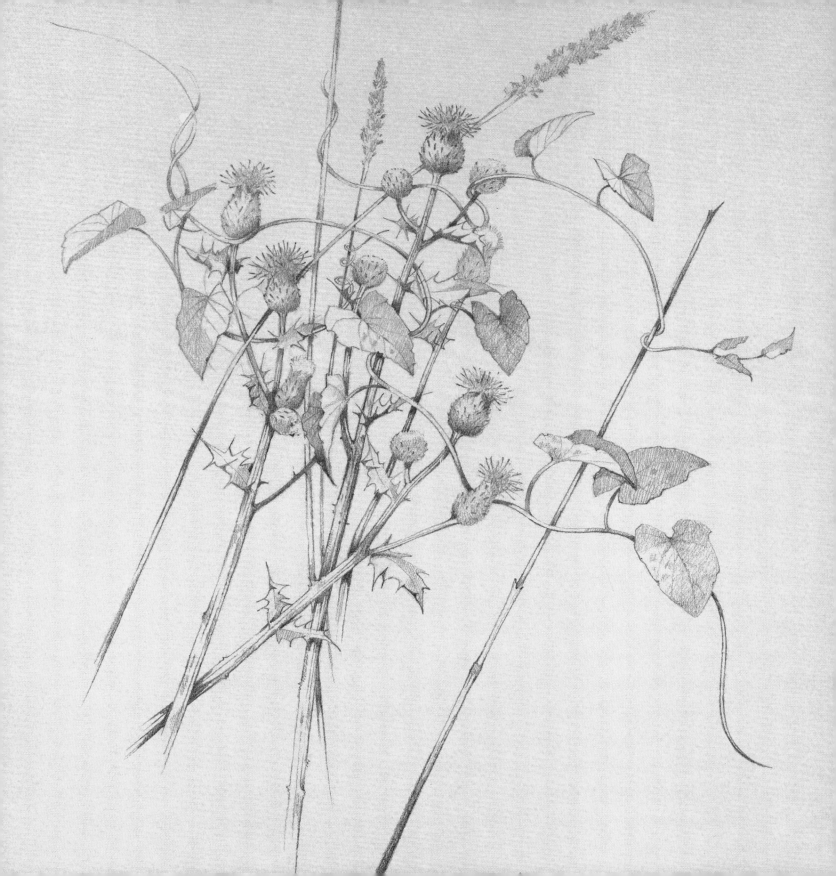

beds in front of the house. Nowadays, the harvest mice have moved away from the cornfields and usually live in the hedgerows. My picture of them with rosehips is not an imaginary scene but was painted from life. The harvest mice have adapted to the fact that cornfields are no longer hospitable places for them, instead of being wiped out like the corncrakes.

Among the most exciting inhabitants of my garden are dormice, which are much less common than they were a few years ago. They were always rather difficult to find, but sometimes you could turn over a log or remove some loose bark from an old tree and find a nest. It does not matter that I have never seen them here, although I shall be very happy when I do get a glimpse of them. For the moment, it is enough that I can find nuts opened with such neat, round holes that I know dormice must have been responsible.

I can also see stoats and weasels, and recently some badgers tried to get into my rabbit hutches. A wild garden attracts a large variety of birds – woodpeckers, nuthatches, treecreepers, warblers, goldcrests and a lot of finches, such as redpolls and siskins, bullfinches and chaffinches. In effect, the garden is an extension of the countryside with a little bit of lawn around the house so that we can get in and out. All I have to do is walk out of the door and my subject is all around me.

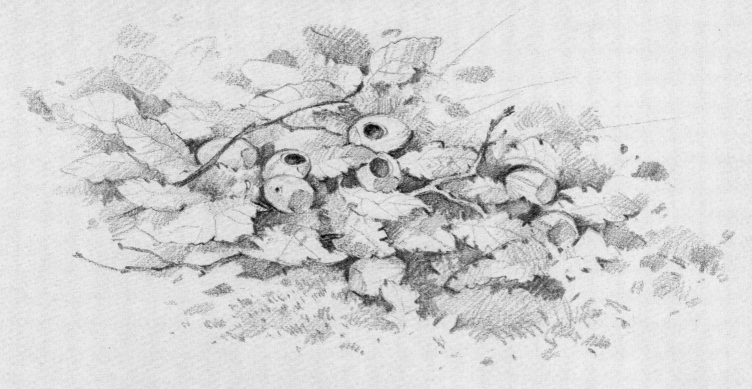

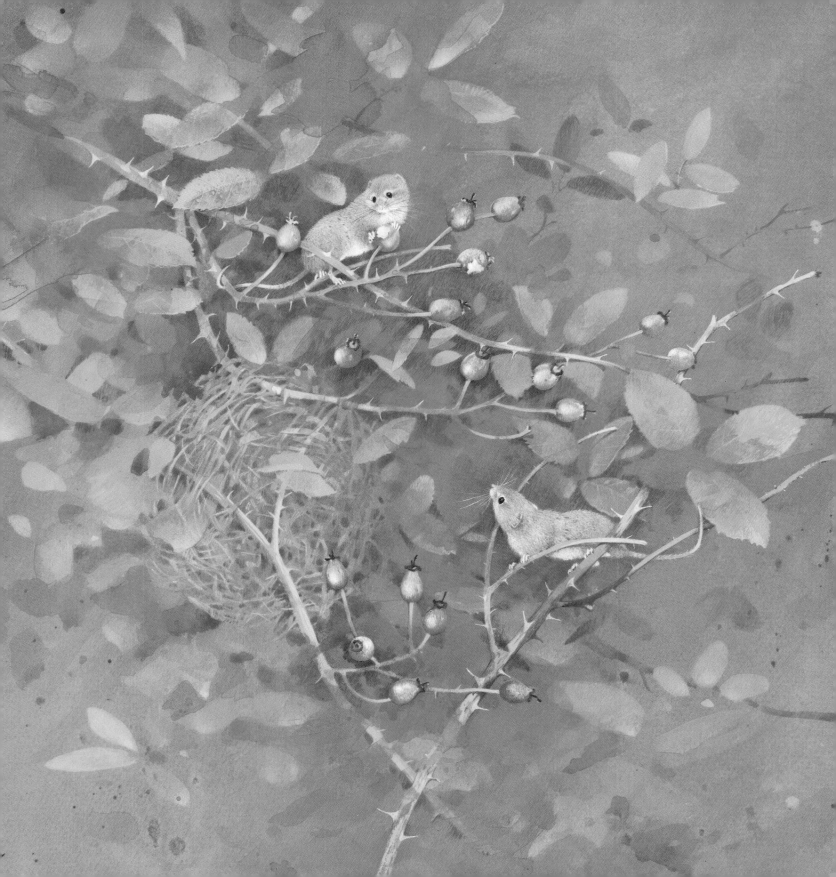

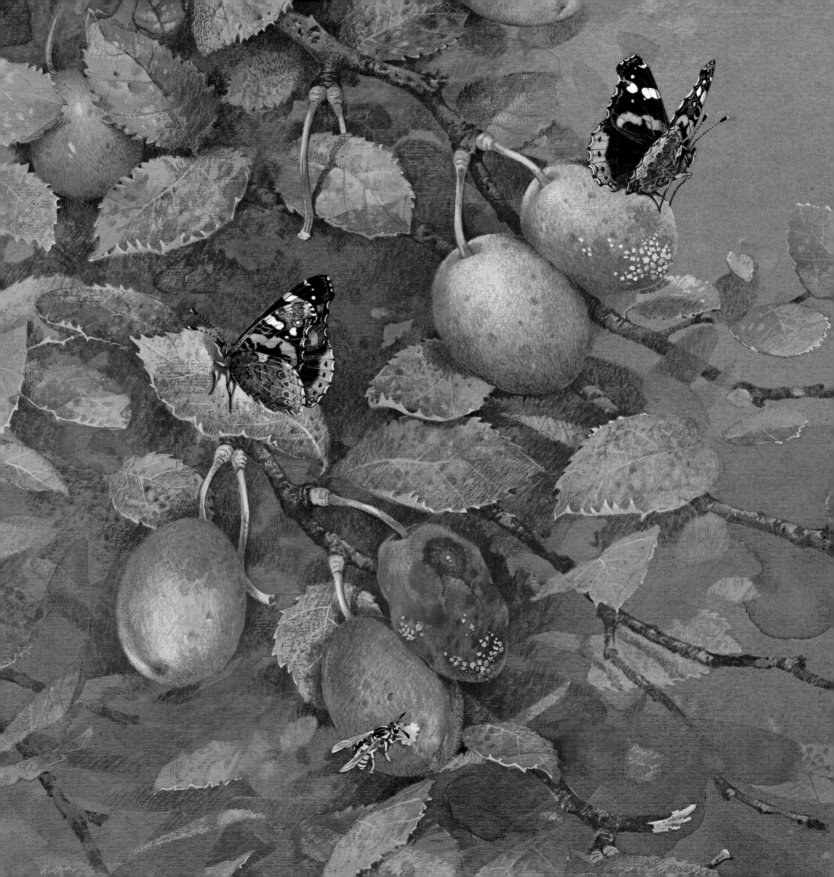

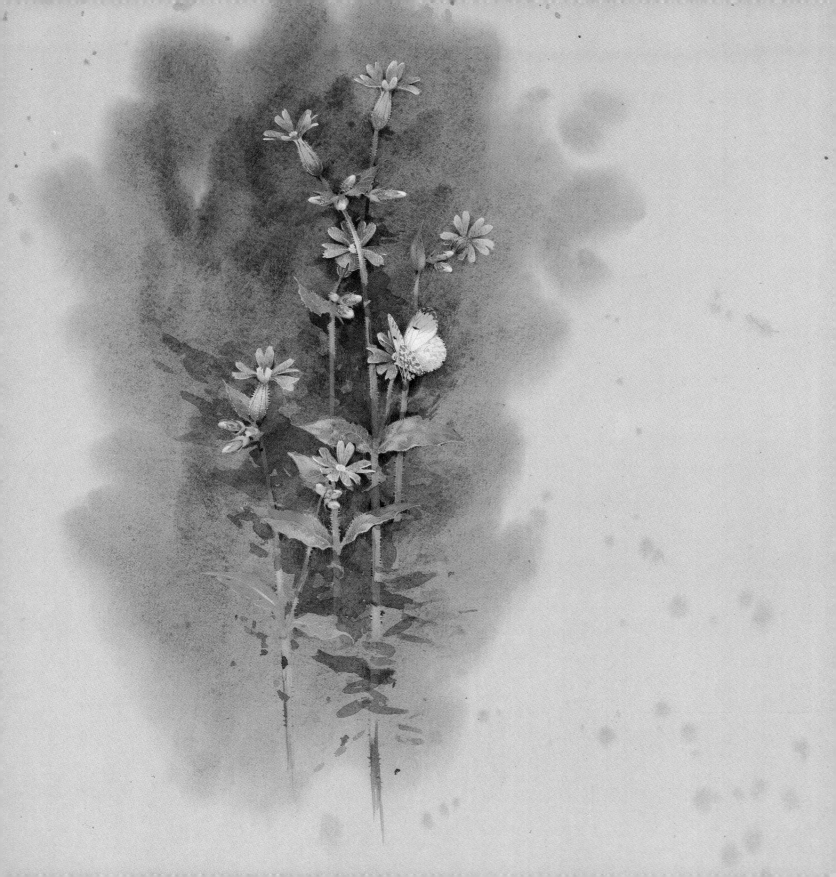

Butterflies

When I started as a wildlife artist, my first subjects were game birds such as pheasants and partridges. From them, I went on to the smaller songbirds and to mammals. However, I have always been attracted by butterflies – I enjoy trying to find aberrations and variations in the different species, and many of my favourite places are good locations for butterflies. I wanted to do something new: to paint them as living creatures in their own world rather than as dead specimens in an identification book. Because butterflies

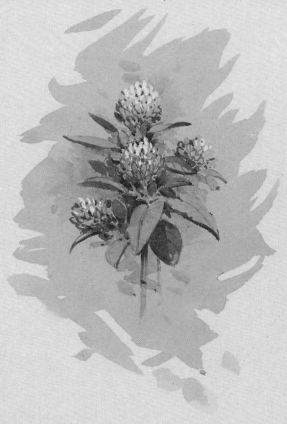

on the whole do not rest with their wings outstretched in the setting board position, my pictures show them as you will see them in nature, perhaps with their wings folded up over their backs, perhaps with no more than a glimpse of the brightly coloured upper side showing.

I spent seven or eight years experimenting with butterfly pictures and developing ways of painting them. This, of course, involved sketching them in the field but also meant my getting down on my hands and knees and crawling around in the butterflies' own environment. Here, as always, I was helped by my overgrown garden. It is a breeding place for peacocks and small tortoiseshells. There are holly blues in the hedgerow and commas that tend to live among the stinging nettles.

The red admirals which I have painted were also near at hand. My neighbour has a fine old Victoria plum tree which produced a splendid crop, so large indeed that there were many more plums than they could use or give away. Quite a number of plums just rotted on the tree and attracted red admirals and wasps, both of which like to feed on rotting fruit in autumn.

On the other hand, the orange tip was not in my garden, although we do see plenty of them in May. The red campion is very much a Dorset flower, which is found all over grassy banks and hedgerows there. The startling colour combination of the orange tip resting on them is not one that I would ever have invented for myself. It is something that I had to see.

Although I am lucky enough to have quite a good cross-section of our butterflies in my garden, it is very obvious to me that there are simply not as many as there were in the past. Even the white butterflies, which used to infest the cabbages are now seen in ones and twos rather than multitudes. It is no exaggeration to say that every species of British butterfly is endangered. Butterflies show their vulnerability even more quickly than birds. They are much more delicate and rely on specific plants for their food; their habitat is only too easily destroyed.

The people who have been in a position to notice the decline in butterfly populations are the collectors. I do not believe that their activities have had

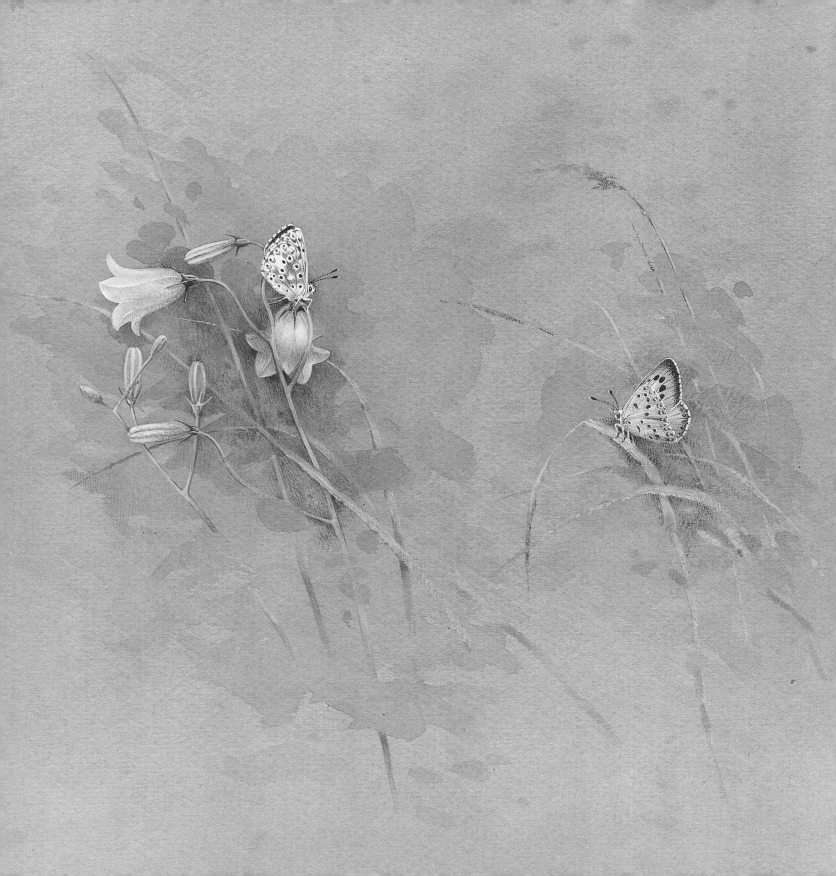

any significant effect on butterfly stocks in Britain except in the case of one or two very rare things like the large copper in the nineteenth century, a species that was made vulnerable in the first place by the draining of the fens that were its habitat. Anyone who has been collecting butterflies since the war can tell you just how much of the countryside that makes a good natural habitat has been destroyed in the past few decades.

The most recent victim has been the large blue, although the chequered skipper now also seems to be doomed in England, even if it survives in Scotland. The large blue has always bred in England, but over the years has become increasingly scarce. Much of its habitat has changed. The life cycle of the large blue involves both wild thyme and a particular ant in whose nests its caterpillars mature. Such a complicated development probably has less chance of success than something more straightforward. Robert Goodden, who tried to save the species in Britain by breeding it in artificial conditions, is still hoping for success in rearing it, and his experiments continue. In 1979, the few large blues that remained in the wild failed to reproduce, and the species is now thought to be extinct in Britain, although it survives in continental Europe.

The butterfly on the left of the painting with the large blue is the chalkhill blue, a species that is restricted to chalk downs. I like it for the beautiful silvery blue colour on the upper side of the male's wings which make a fine sight when it settles on a harebell. The chalkhill blue is also fascinating because it is the most variable of all British butterflies – collectors have devoted their lives to finding aberrations of it. But you can observe these by walking across the downs on a dull day and looking at the butterflies resting in the grass – there is no problem in getting close enough to study them.

I have never seen a large blue alive, and my picture uses information taken from a cabinet specimen. It shows the butterfly as I would like to have seen it – something I will probably never have the chance to do, at least in Britain. It is my visual epitaph for a lost species.

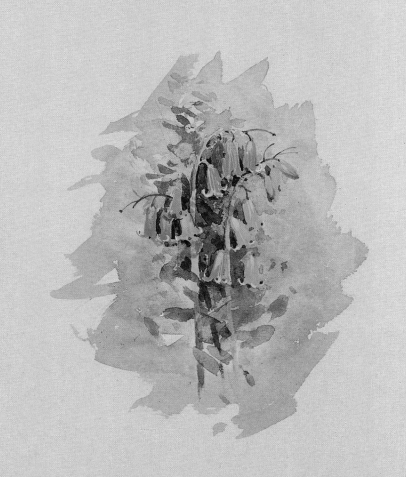

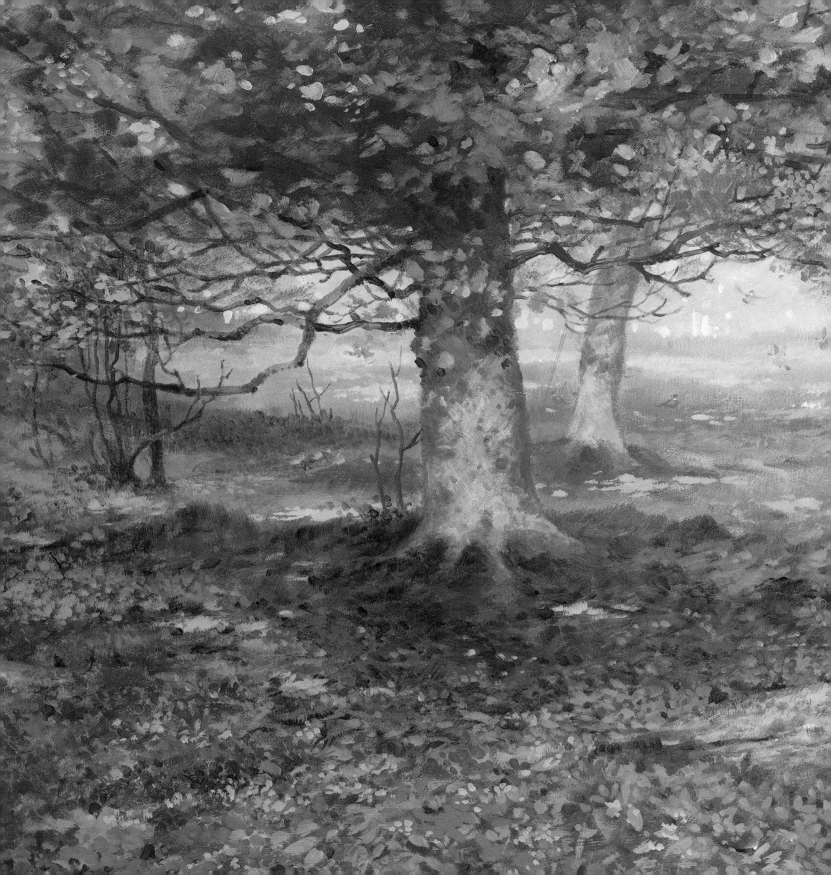

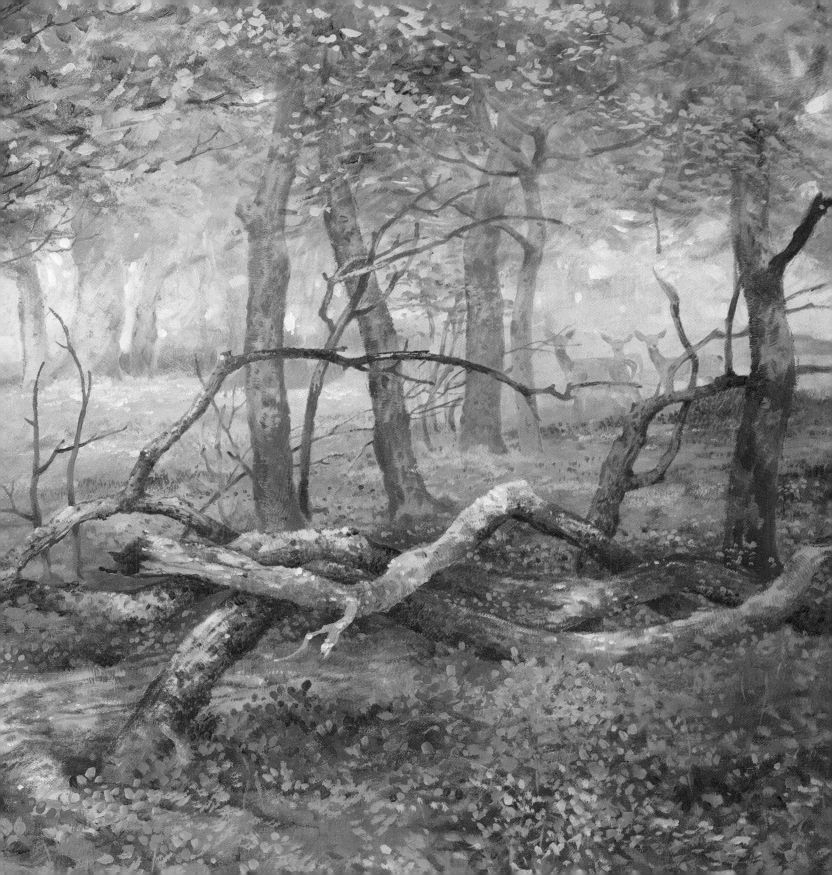

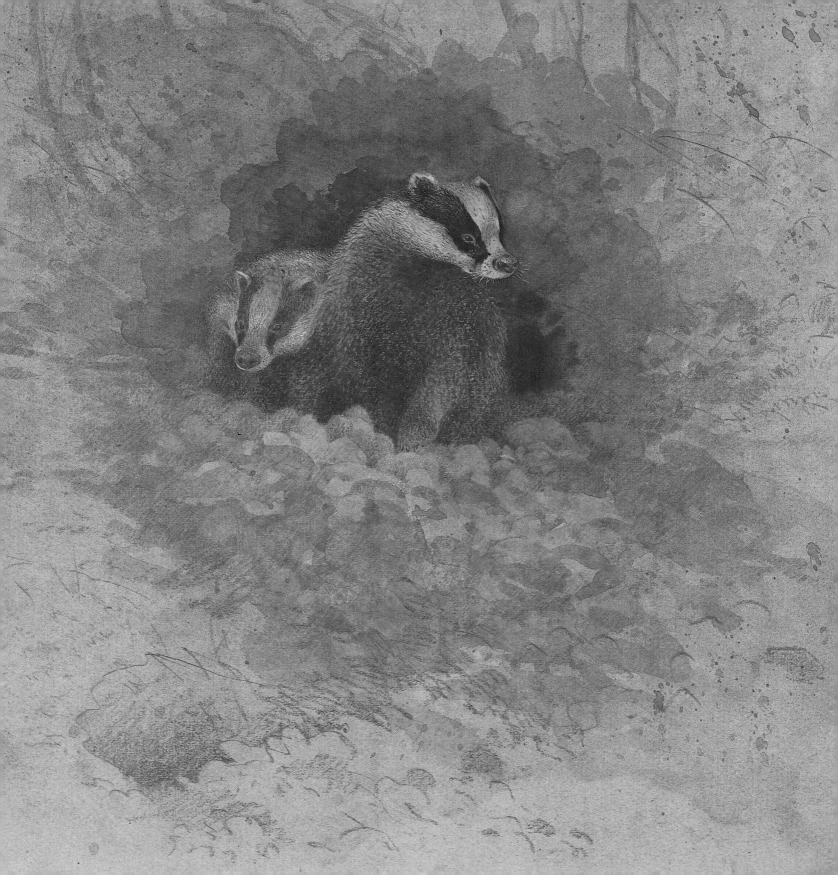

Woodlands

The woodland around here is predominantly beech. In the distant past, the whole area was a vast beech forest, of which strong evidence still remains, notably in the large expanse of Ashridge. This old estate is in the main solid beech forest, but intermixed with a variety of other trees plus, inevitably, some conifer plantations. Like most wooded areas of Britain, this one finds itself with many very old trees that are approaching the end of their life cycle. Enough of the beeches here, though, have a long life ahead of them to prevent the forest disappearing for many years, during which time we must make sure that there is replanting on a massive scale. The National Trust has a scheme well under way, but, as a fanatic on this subject, I believe that there is no limit to the number of trees that can usefully be planted. At the moment, I am fairly hopeful for trees in this part of Hertfordshire.

However, one sort of replanting horrifies me: the hacking down of our mixed woodlands and their replacement by spruces and Christmas trees which are useless as a habitat for wildlife. While the trees are tiny, a mass of plants such as bramble and rosebay willow herb can grow up between them, but as the trees become larger, they inexorably blot out the light and obliterate all the undergrowth. The result is to increase the pressure on our vanishing habitats. Today's foresters are quite likely to hack out the heart of a wood, leave a respectable-looking fringe of deciduous trees round the edge and grow the Christmas trees in the middle. On Forestry Commission land, you are likely to see nothing except trees.

The older forests have suffered from being tidied up and generally rationalized. The rides have been cleared out and machinery has been used to tear out the brambles. The New Forest, which used to be a crucial area for the preservation of endangered butterfly species, is rapidly becoming

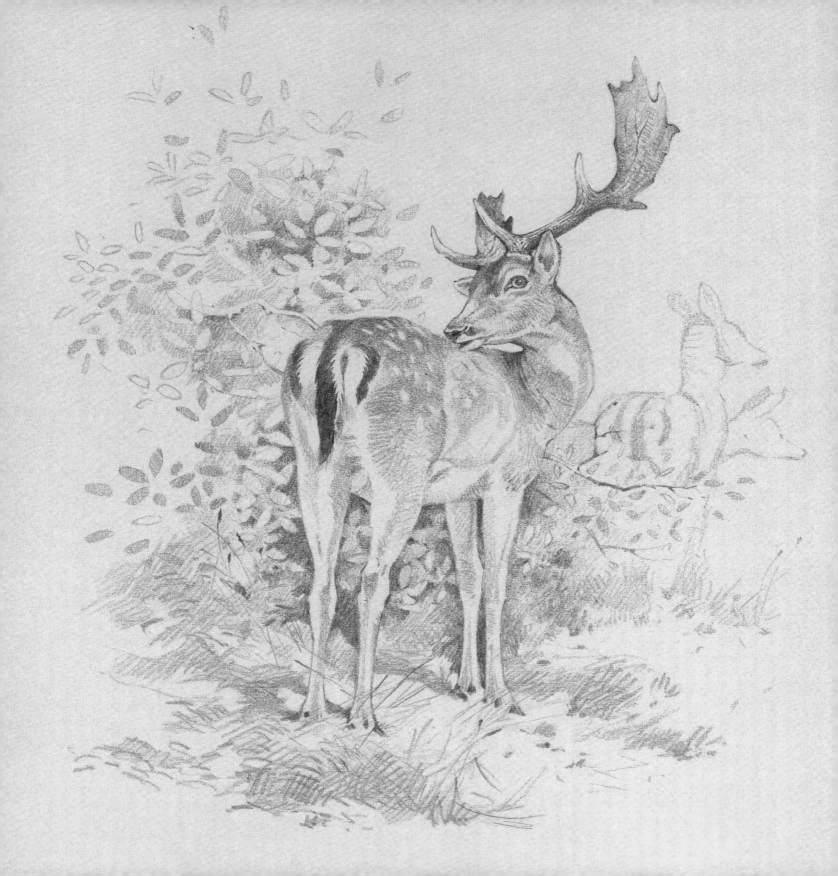

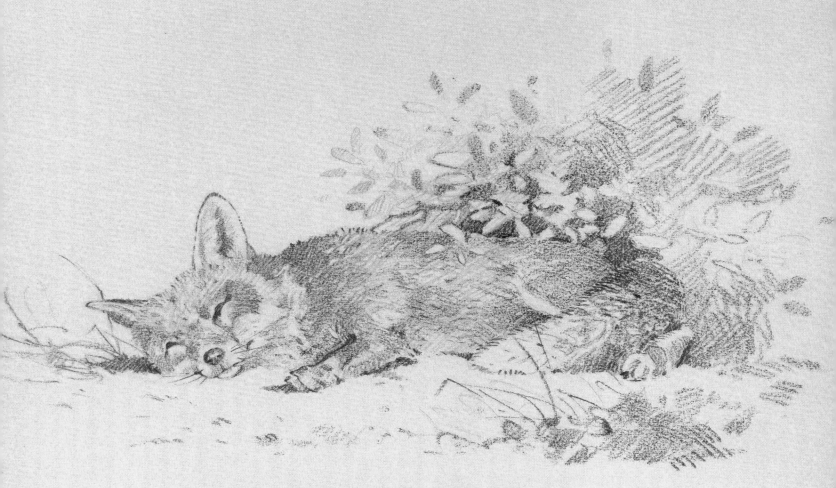

entirely useless because of the intensive tidying up. The reverse process happened during the war, when the butterflies did very well because the woodlands and hedgerows were left alone.

Forests like Ashridge provide the habitat for some of our larger mammals: badgers, foxes and deer. The fox I have drawn is relaxing but still alert. Foxes have an extraordinary ability to snatch some sleep at any time while keeping one eye open to see what is going on. They love sunning themselves like that during the day. I find them in my little orchard – they lie in the tall, dry grass or tuck themselves into a sunny spot under the hedgerow. Badgers, on the other hand, are more or less nocturnal creatures and I have shown them coming out to forage at twilight, perhaps from one of the many well-established old sets that there are in nearby woodlands. They had probably been around my acre of land for a long time before their efforts to get into my rabbit hutches showed me that they were there.

Both of our species of deer have been introduced, but at very different times. As this part of Hertfordshire does not seem to have any roe deer, our small deer are muntjaks, which are relatively recent escapes from captivity that have established themselves in our woodlands. Although they are aliens, I do not object to their presence at all. They are attractive creatures, about the size of a large dog, and do not cause enough damage to be worth worrying about. In fact, I would be happy to see more of them. We are so short of wildlife that they can only enhance the countryside.

However, it is the fallow deer that I want to portray because it is so much a part of the countryside here. Fallow deer were traditionally kept for hunting, and for hundreds of years there have been large herds both at Ashridge and on the Halsey estate, which goes back to the fifteenth century and was developed for sport until just after the First World War. This is an area of big estates – one joins the next all the way from here to the Chilterns. From the woodlands, the herds of fallow deer also move out across the fields. In my drawing, the stag is having a little preen, and there is a suggestion of some hinds just moving off in the background.

I have also put a glimpse of deer into my large painting of a typical piece of Ashridge at bluebell time, in May. I have tried to show the clean, pearly atmosphere which the forest has in the morning. The deer have just seen me and are about to move off; in a moment, they will have disappeared altogether. I wanted to convey the feeling that the wildlife is not at all obvious in the countryside, that it is just a piece of luck that it has appeared at this moment. You have to look for the deer in the picture just as you would in a forest.

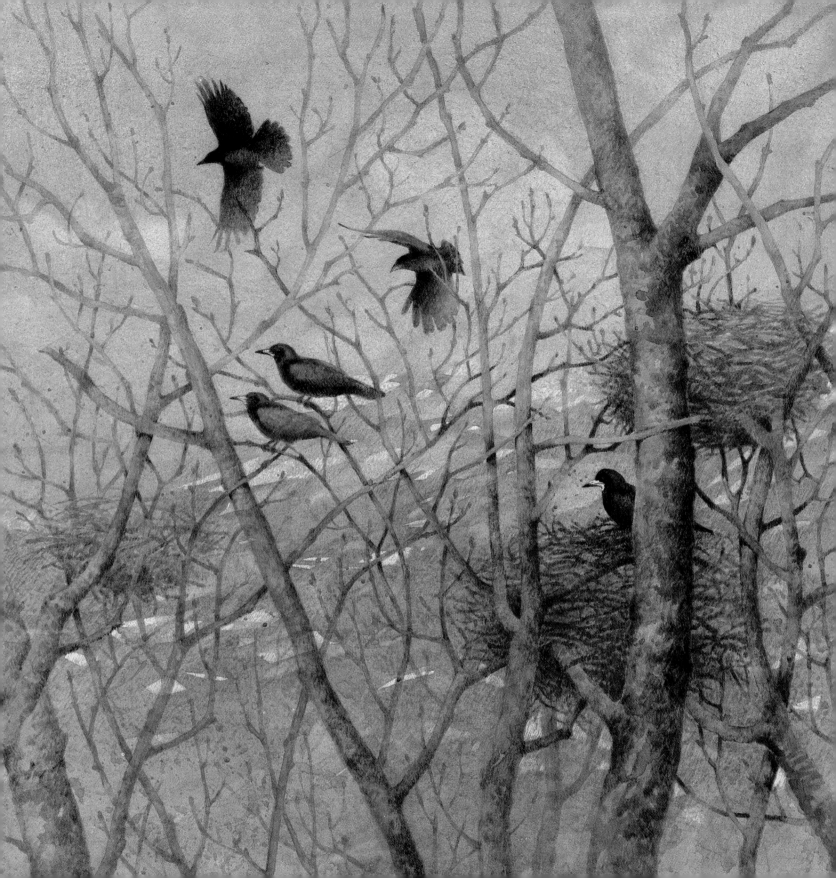

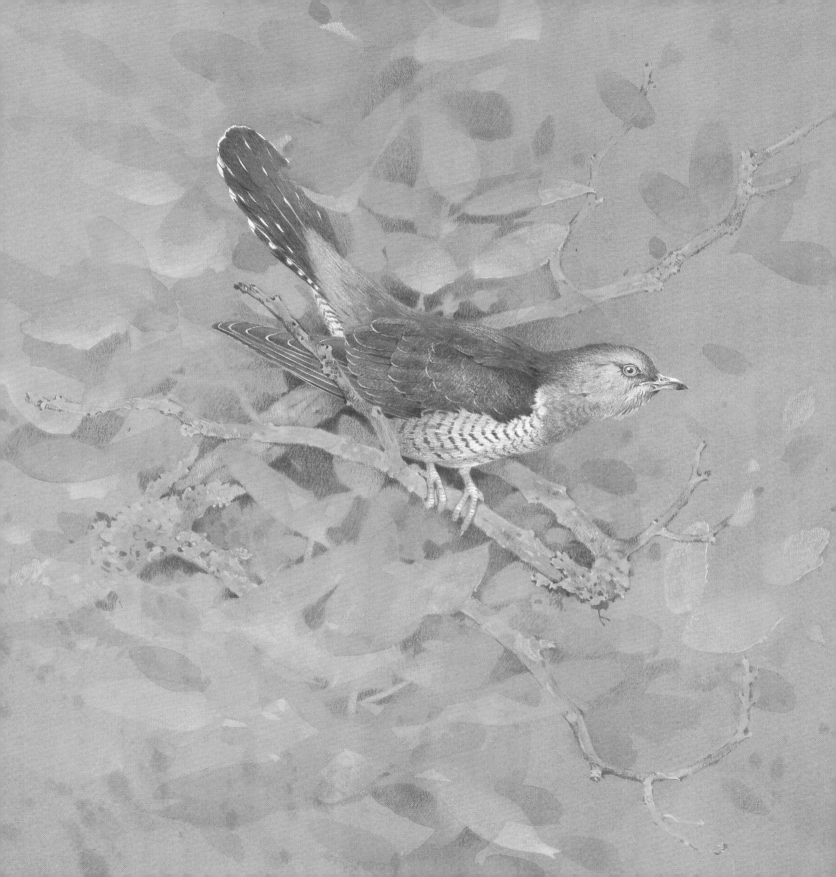

The most conspicuous birds that nest in our woodlands – if only because of the noise they make – are the rooks. It goes without saying, though, that their numbers are greatly reduced both because of the loss of many of the trees that were their nesting sites and perhaps because of the changes in land use. I can see no justification now for the traditional activity of rook shooting. As far as I can see, the birds do more good than harm, although they do turn the seed over in spring, which is, I suppose, what worries the farmers. My rook picture was painted in March, when the trees were still bare and the rooks were therefore very conspicuous in their tree tops. In February and March, they start to get interested in rebuilding their nests; it is a time when they are very busy and noisy. During the early evening they make an extraordinary din, and as you look up you can see the last glimmers of light forming the background against which they lift off from the branches. The birds from the rookery across the river fly over to feed on the fields behind my cottage.

A woodland bird that we hear very much more often than we see it is the cuckoo. Everyone in the countryside likes to hear its call, which is one of the loveliest and most evocative sounds of spring and early summer. Because our area is quite heavily wooded, we still have a good number of cuckoos but certainly nowhere near as many as their were when I was at school – then, during May and June, their sound could be heard all the time. The position of the cuckoo in my picture is very characteristic: leaning forward with the tail rather high. It has short, stubby legs and a long tail that always seems to be waving from side to side or up and down.

Some birds demand to be painted in a particular season, even though I may see them throughout the year. One such is the woodcock, which breeds in the woods on the local estates, where it is always quite common. When I have been out walking, I have seen as many as four or five during a day. It is above all their colour, ranging from cream to dark brown, that attracts me and makes me want to portray them among the browns of autumnal woodland.

The woodcock is a rather personal symbol of autumn, but woodlands offer many more commonplace, but nevertheless evocative, autumnal images. Toadstools are among my favourites, both for their colours and for their fairy-tale associations. The fly agarics, which are the red ones with white spots, are not as fussy as many fungi about where they grow; you will find them in oak as well as beech woods. For some reason, they seem to provoke people to kick them and break them up; it is as if they are somehow frightening, whether because they are poisonous or because they perhaps look a little evil, or even because they have associations with witchcraft and the supernatural.

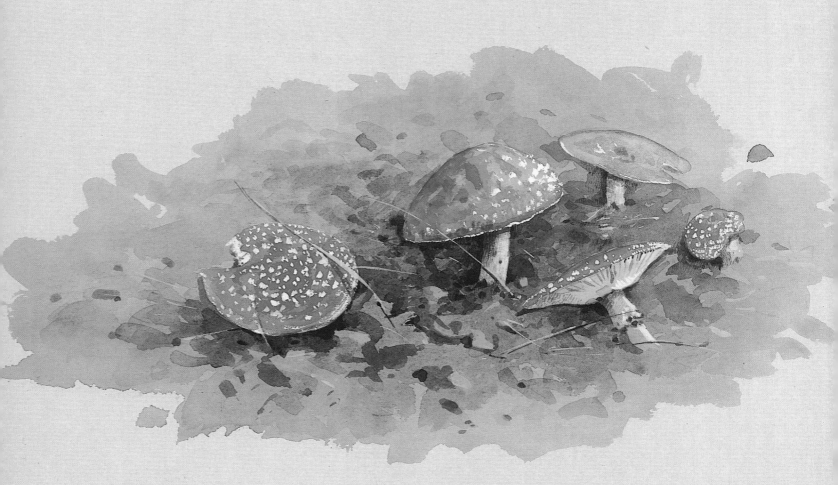

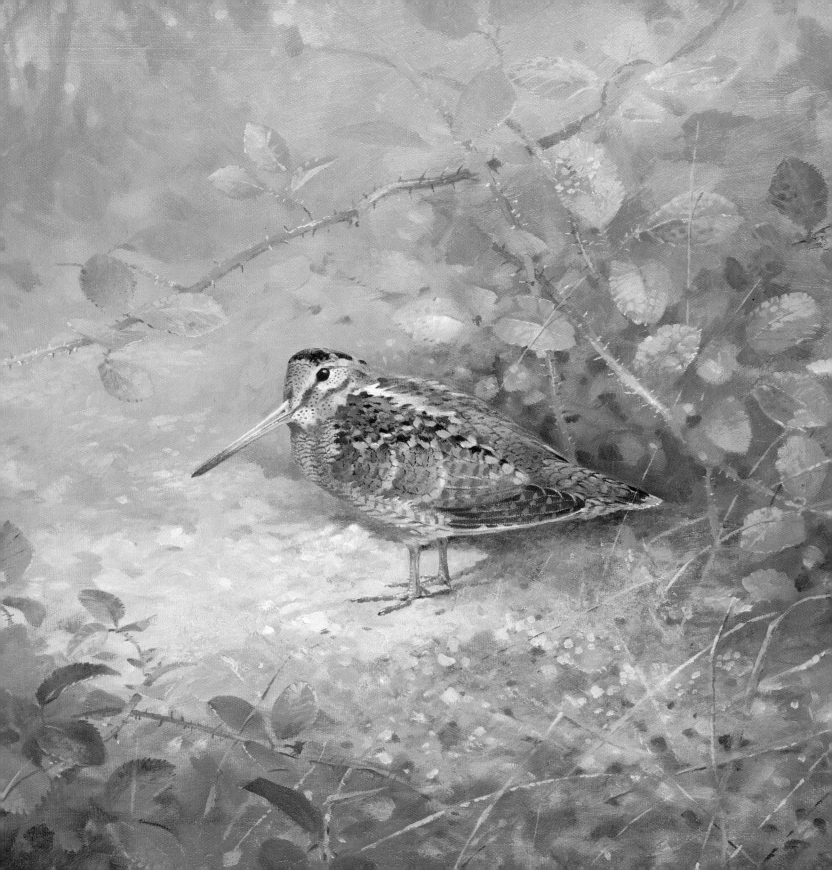

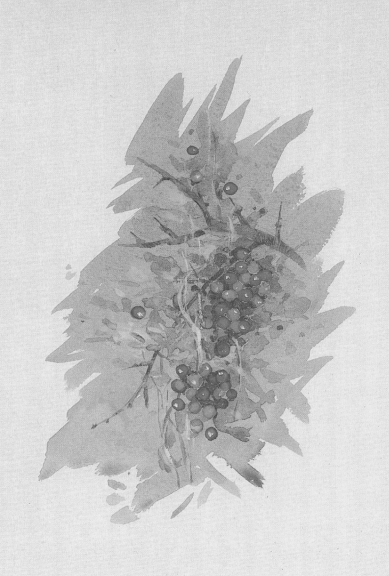

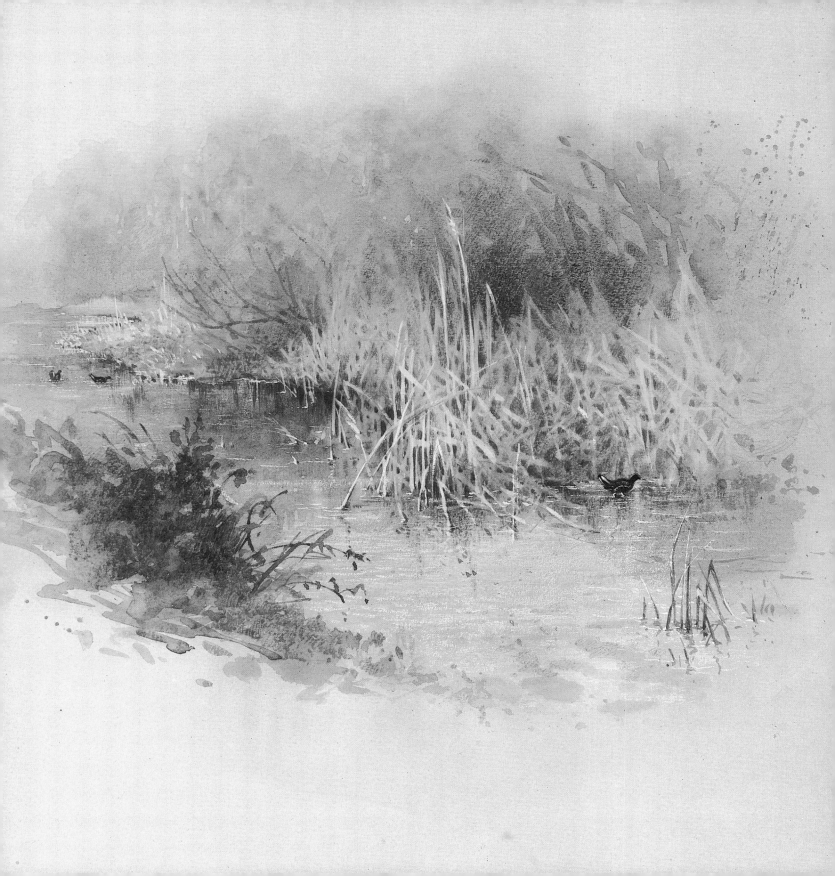

Ponds and Streams

Neither Hertfordshire nor Dorset has very much open water; they are not counties with large lakes or majestic rivers, although Dorset does have the sea. The lack of open water makes our small ponds and streams all the more precious. The tiny stone footbridge I have painted is in Dorset. It leads to a farm and is only just wide enough to walk across. It is over a ditch leading to a stream by a village that I know well. I have often walked past and have occasionally wondered if the bridge was gradually falling apart. However, I am sure that it has already survived for a very long time – it would have been built specially for the farmhouse.

Western Hertfordshire has very few chalk streams, one of which runs in front of my cottage. It rises as a spring only a short distance away, just above the village, and is mainly bordered by meadows, so that it is unpolluted and free from old tin cans and abandoned bedsteads. If it were any less clean, the trout would not thrive in it as they do.

The river is stocked and fished by a group of twenty-five of us, most of whom are interested in natural history. We have managed to keep it as a genuinely rural river with reed beds and thick undergrowth on the banks hanging over into the water. I think that most of us would hate it to become smart and tidy. I have seen some river banks that have been civilized for the benefit of the anglers by being mown and having park benches placed at regular intervals along them. On the Gade, you have to pick your way through nettles and thistles and reeds, which is as it should be. We always maintain that, although we enjoy the fishing, our main aim has to be the preservation of the river bank environment.

If we hacked everything down and made the river bank into a lawn, there would be no cover for the animal life of the river. Frogs, for example, do not just need water – they have to have plenty of shady, damp cover, which they also find in the jungle area around my house. I like to think that an

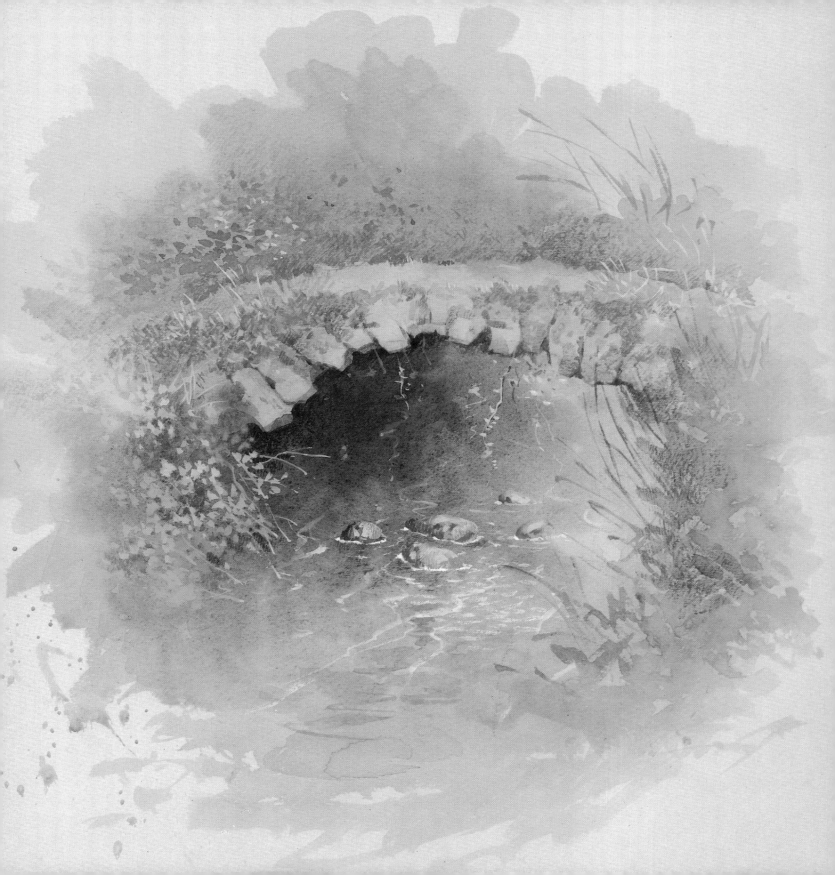

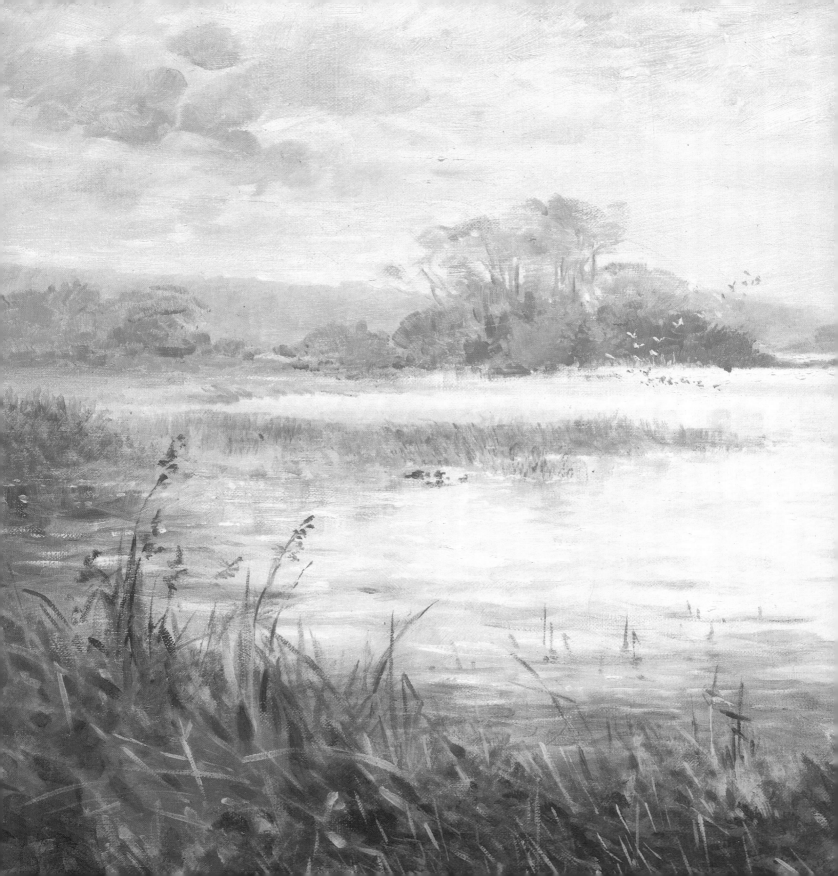

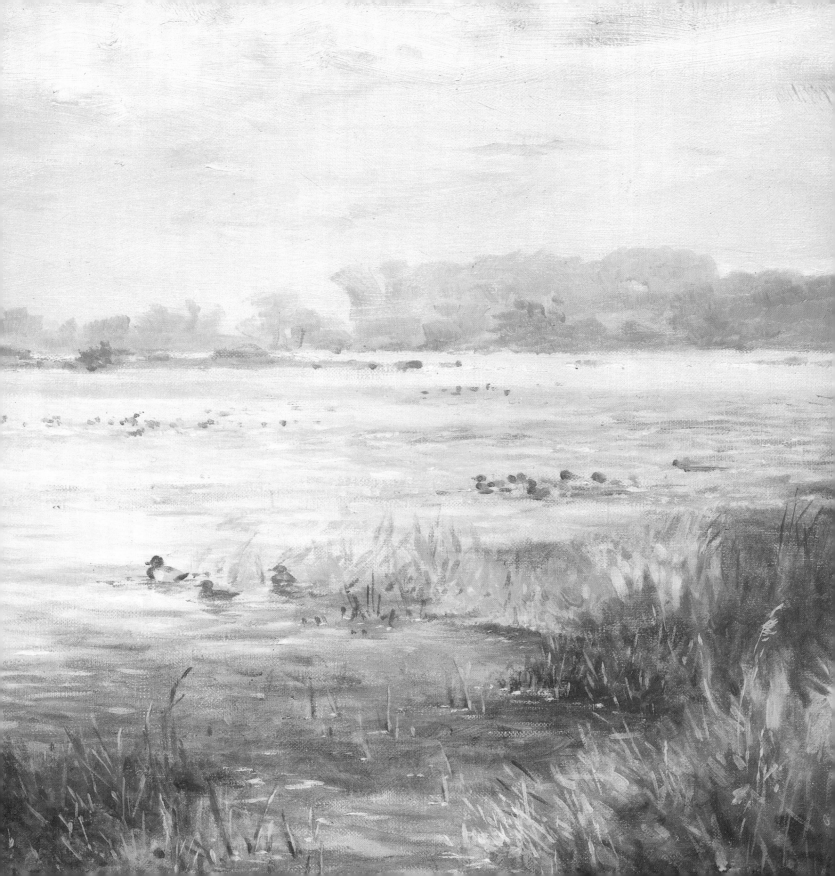

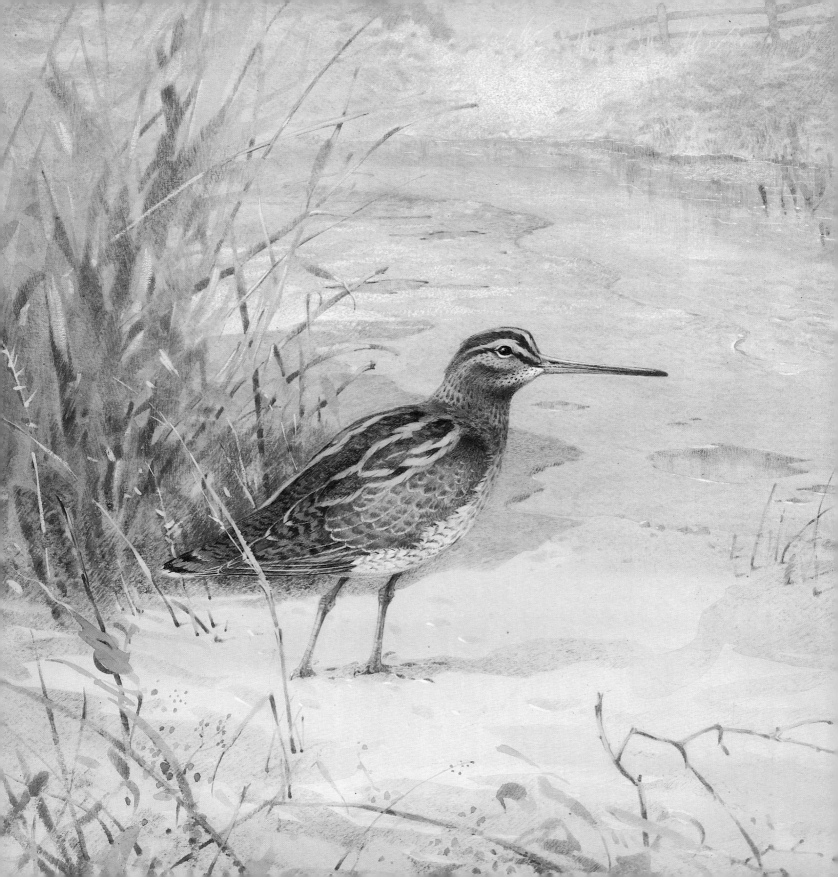

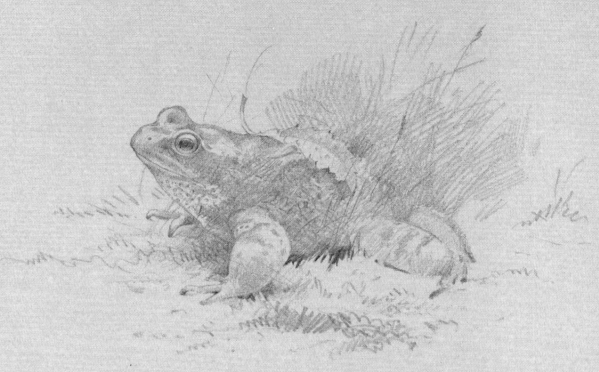

indication of our success is that a couple of years ago a bittern stayed on the river bank for about ten days. We also have kingfishers, as well as water rail, which are notoriously shy birds that skulk in the vegetation like the one I have painted.

The picture of the snipe was the first that I produced specially for this book. During the winter months, snipe are present in large numbers along the river; some of them stay throughout the year and nest near by. They feed on the margins between the reed beds and the water where they can probe with their long bills. Any muddy corner on the water's edge can contain a snipe. In the winter, you will also see them out on the open water meadows where there are pools, as there often are in the marshy fields of the valley in which the Gade runs. Although they are quite common, they are rather easily frightened, and it is fairly difficult to get close to snipe on the ground. To make the sketches for this picture, I just sat down quietly on the river bank and waited for the snipe to come back.

75

I can observe water voles almost any time I walk along the river bank. As far as I can see, they are totally harmless. The only thing that could possibly be held against them is that they burrow into the banks and make holes. When you are sitting fishing, you may see their chubby little faces as they swim past – a charming sight. Water voles can apparently be found in meadows, even at some distance from water, but I always think of them as river creatures, if only for their associations with *The Wind in the Willows*. On one occasion, about three years ago, as I was walking along the bank of the Gade, I caught sight of a water vole sitting in the crook of a bough just above the level of the water and nibbling at a piece of vegetation. I watched

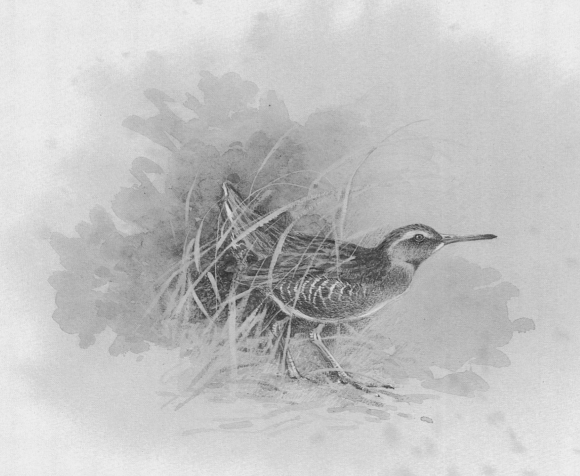

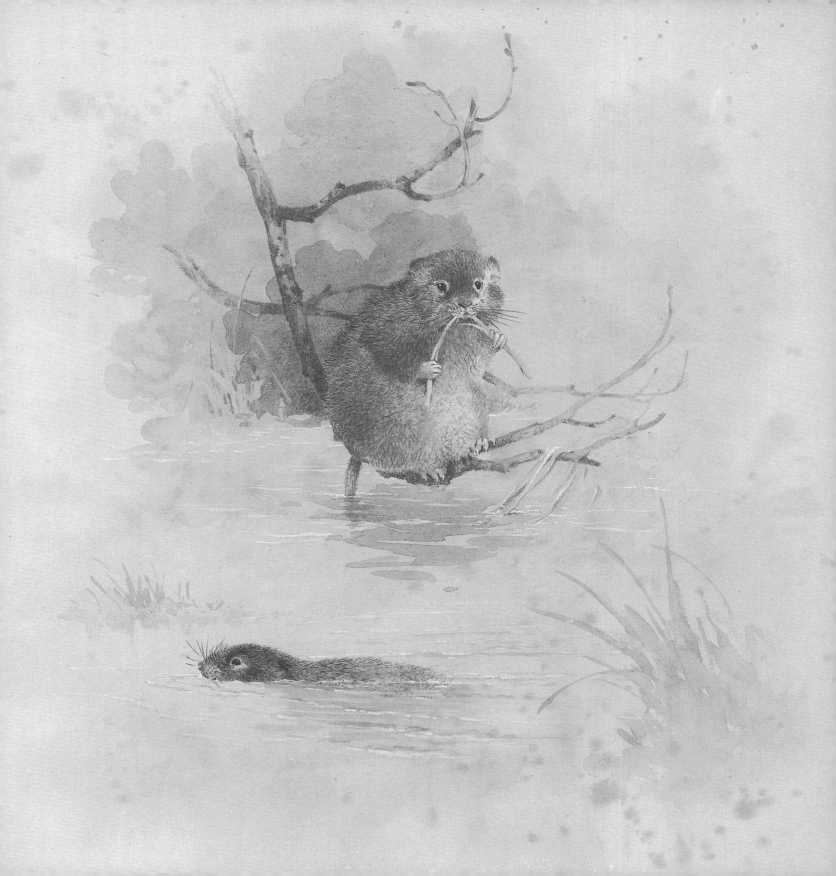

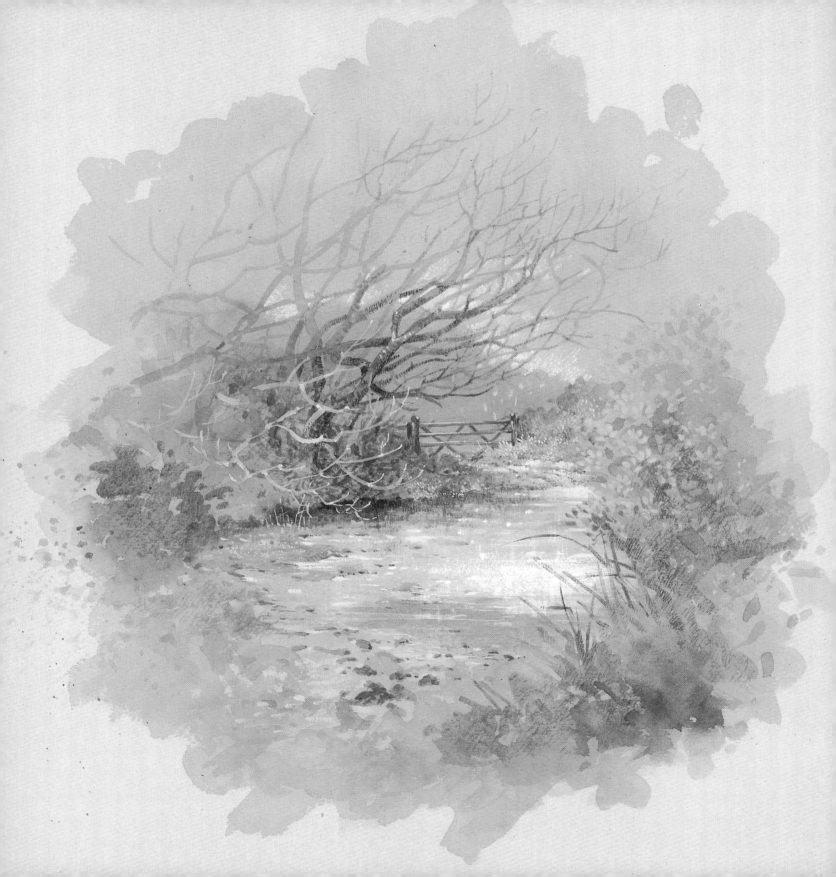

it for a minute or two before it just rolled off like a parachutist leaving an aeroplane and swam away. The image of the water vole in the branch has stayed in my mind ever since as something that I wanted to paint.

Although chalk streams like the Gade have often stayed clean and un-polluted, if only because of the fishing that they offer, ponds are an en-dangered phenomenon. Quite a number of village ponds have survived, complete with ducks and water lilies, but the small ones in the corners of fields, which for me are the most evocative of childhood memories, have mostly disappeared. Many of them have been filled in, and others are so full of chemicals and assorted refuse that they are now dead and fetid. It is difficult now to find a pond to paint that looks as if it might be teeming with frogs and newts, and have dragonflies zooming above it and warblers in the shrubby vegetation on its edges.

The only large stretches of open water in Hertfordshire are the man-made reservoirs and gravel pits. Where these have been in existence for a long time, so that they have become weathered and plenty of trees and natural vegetation have grown up around them, they can be quite an acceptable part of the landscape. The reservoirs that were constructed at Tring in the early nineteenth century to feed the Grand Union Canal have become such good places for wildfowl that they are now a National Nature Reserve and a popular haunt of ornithologists. It was at Tring in 1938 that the little ringed plover bred for the first known time in Britain.

My large picture of Tring shows it on a windy day in March. Around the shores are reeds still standing from the previous year, and in the foreground there is a small group of pochard. Further away, there are larger flocks of duck that are not identifiable to the naked eye. On the far side, you can just see some gulls wheeling around. In the distance is the edge of the Chiltern Hills.

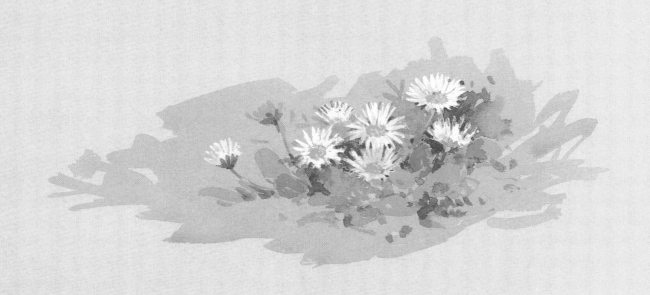

Owls

Owls are among my favourite bird subjects. Each of the three species that I see has a different personality and a different appeal to me. Unfortunately, it is now something of an event to see a barn owl in Hertfordshire, and it is reduced in numbers in the rest of the country. In part, it has suffered in the same way as many other bird predators, but I am not the first to notice one particular factor that works against the barn owl: modern farm buildings are not designed to cater for it. Old barns were often built with access at the top and a platform for the barn owl to breed on because the farmers wanted it there to keep the mice down. Nowadays, we have different methods of getting rid of mice and we see far fewer barn owls. The tawny owl, which is a woodland bird, does not seem to have suffered as severely.

Although most barn owls nest in buildings, including church towers, they will also nest in trees, such as a particular old oak tree I know that is tucked away in a secret spot in the Dorset countryside. You can approach it through deep bracken and observe the birds quite easily through binoculars. The entrance to the hole is in the scar where a large branch has fallen away from the trunk. There are breast feathers where the owls have been standing at the entrance to their home, and of course there are owl pellets made up of the indigestible parts of their prey. This is a storybook tree – the kind that would house Walt Disney's Wise Old Owl – and so appropriate for its use that I am almost as excited by seeing the feathers as I am by seeing an owl. For this reason, I chose not to put the owl into the picture, which has, I hope, a rather nostalgic feeling through being sketched in very faded colours – almost in monochrome.

The barn owls that I have portrayed are in Dorset, where I can see them cruising over their territory at dusk, perhaps coming down the valley from their nesting tree when I am going out to watch badgers. The barn owl in my painting is perching on an old hunt gate in the early dusk. This picture

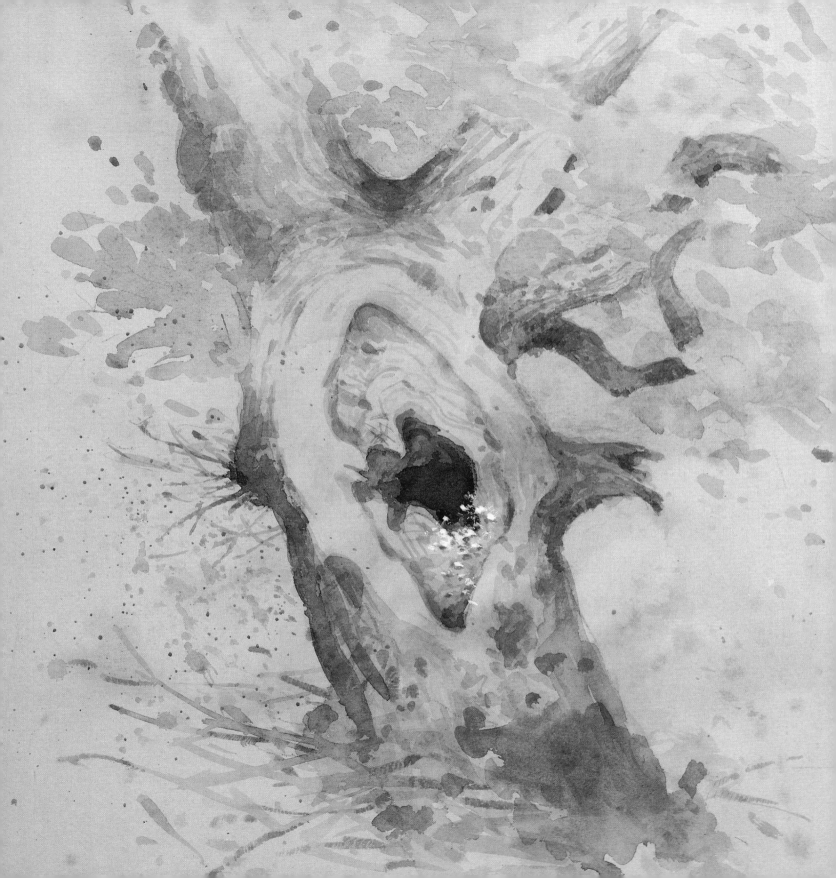

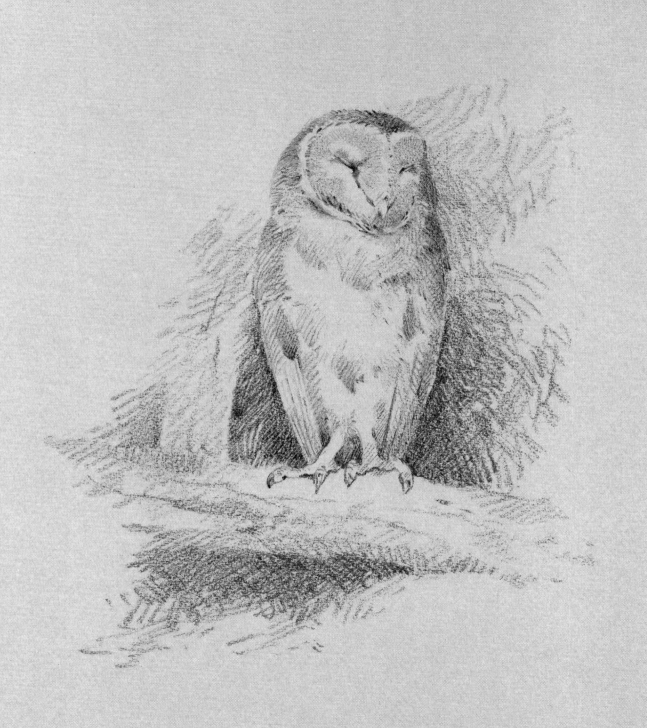

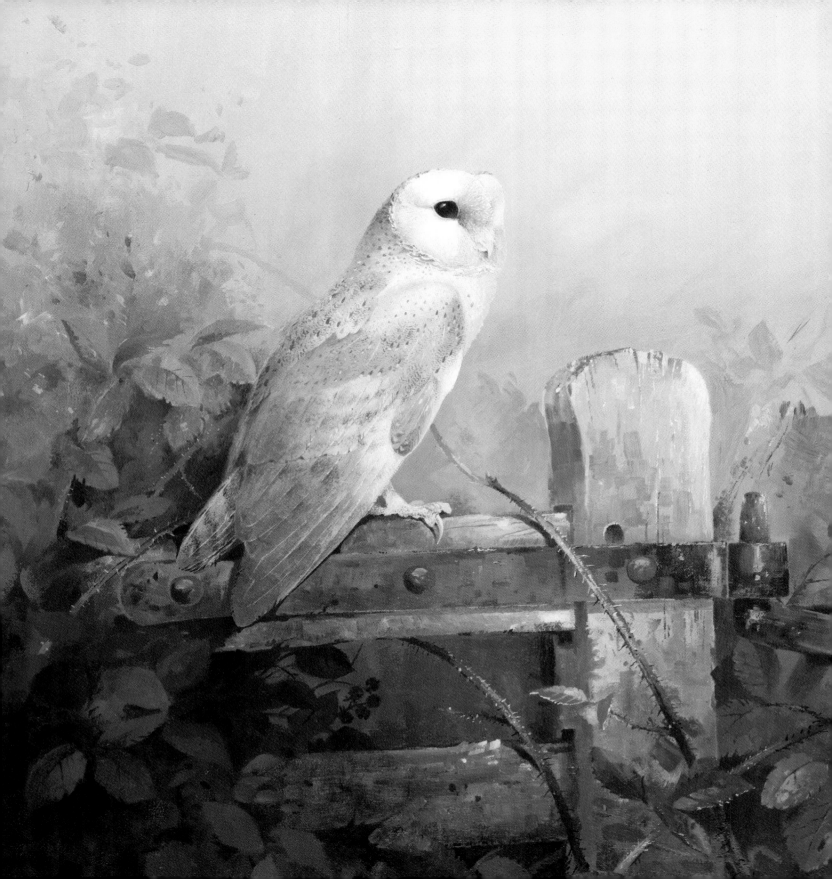

has been made by putting the elements together to produce an image that I have not seen but would like to. The barn owl in the drawing is sleeping during the day in the dark corner of a barn.

The tawny is by far the most common of our owls. A good way of seeing it during the day is to look for the largest holly bush you can find in a wood. If you peer up inside through the dark green leaves, you may see one tucked up against the main stem. Very often, all that is visible is its head; the rest will be shrouded in foliage – hence the treatment of my tawny owl painting, in which the bird is shown in combination with colours that I find pleasing. I have eliminated green, which in any case would not have a great impact in the murky light inside the bush.

The little owl was not introduced into Britain until the late nineteenth century, but has become established throughout much of England and fits into the countryside very well. Unlike the barn owl and the tawny owl, it does not hide away and emerge at twilight. You can see it marauding along the hedgerows at any time of the day. It does not have the same soft, dark eyes as the barn owl and the tawny owl, but has rather sharp, yellow ones, a bit like those of the sparrowhawk.

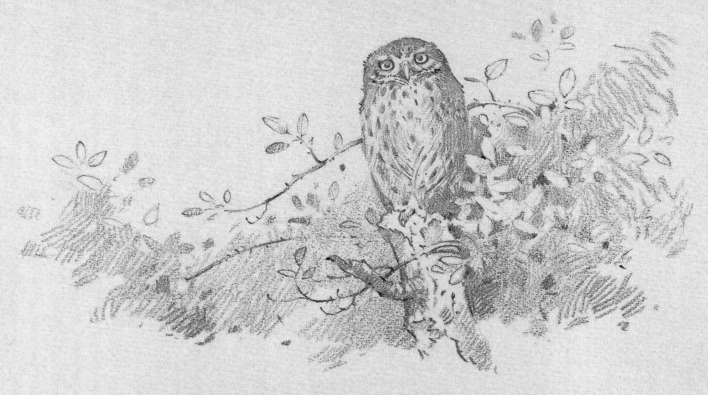

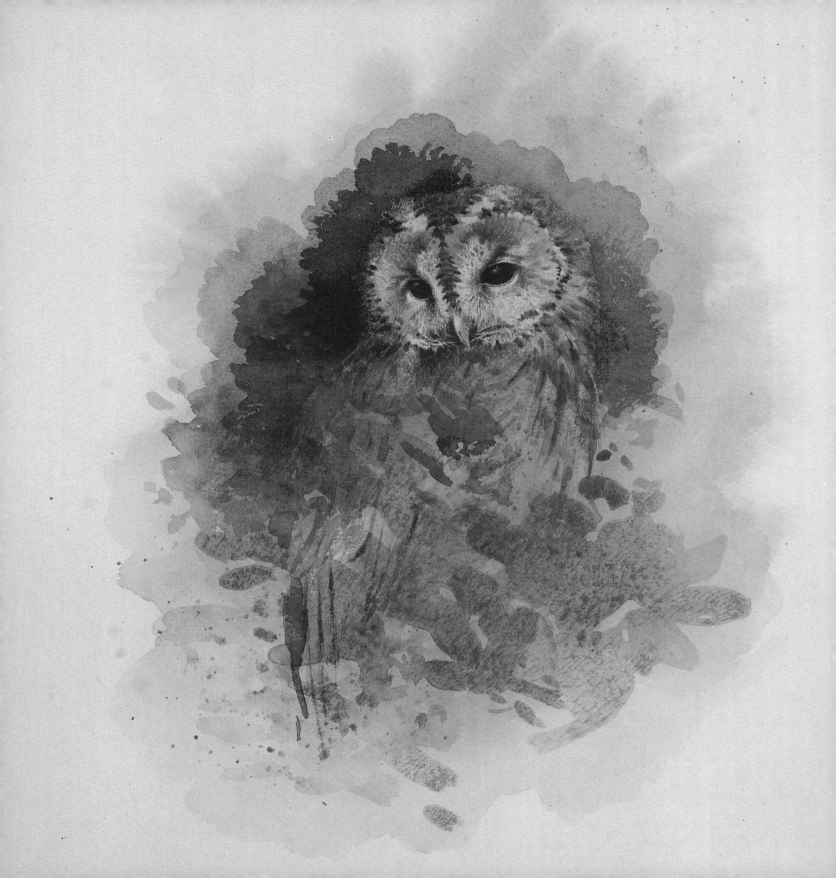

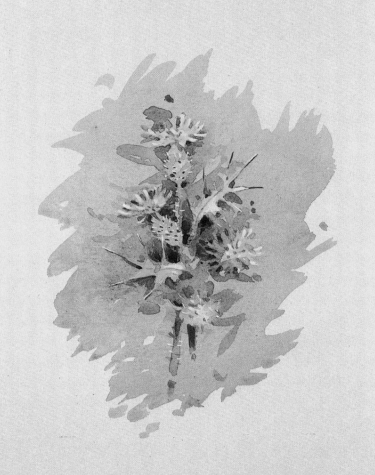

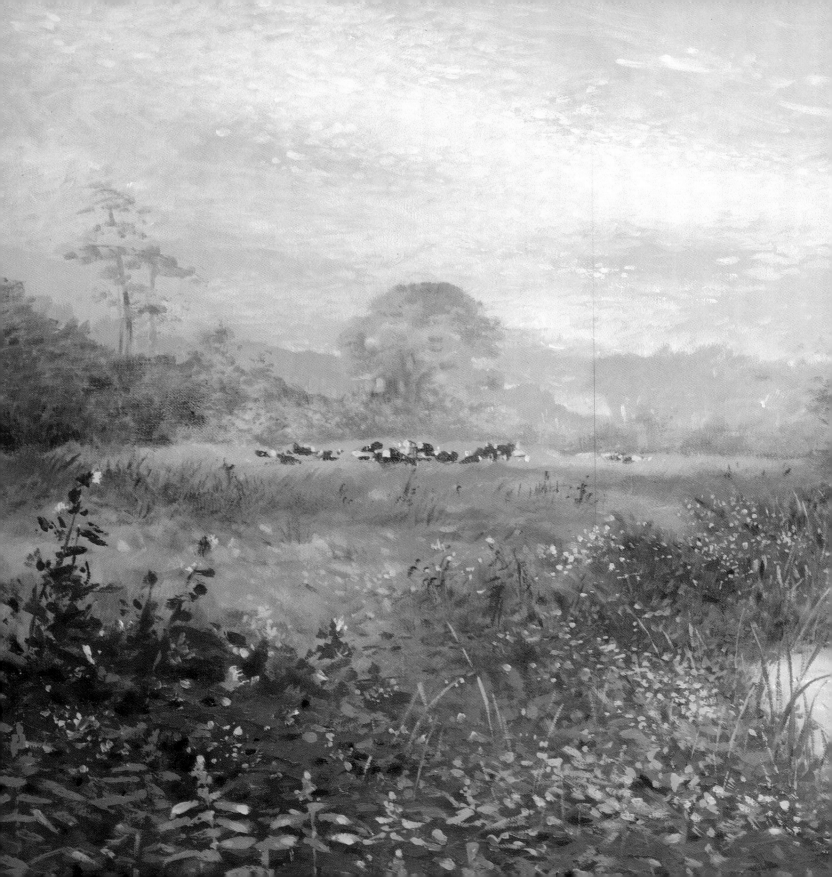

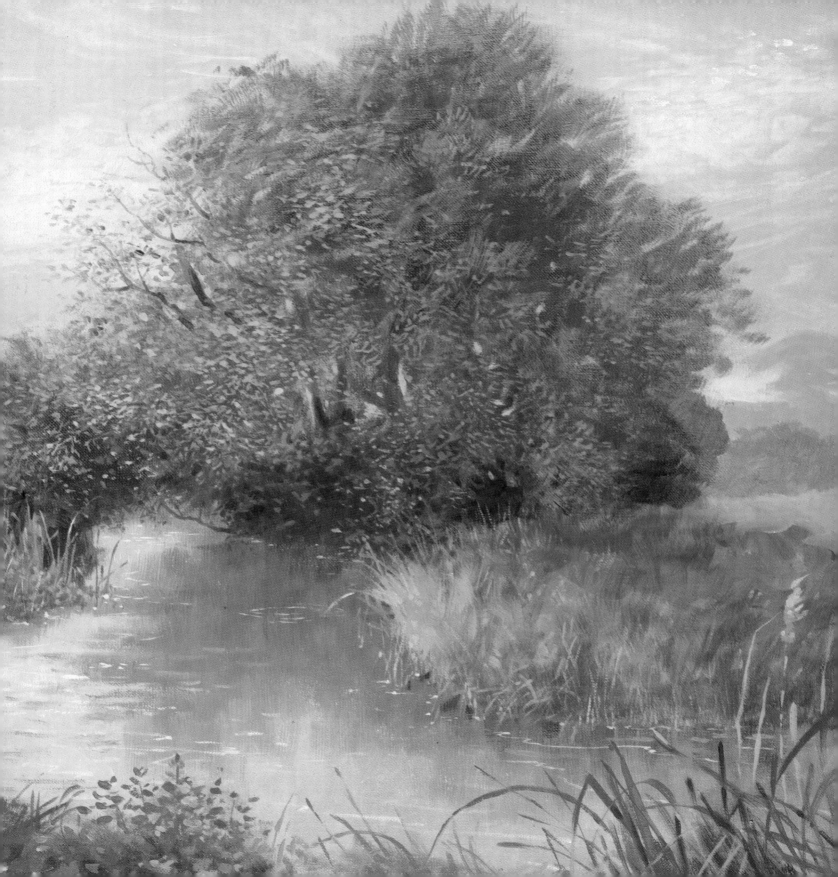

Fields and Hedgerows

The large picture of water meadows represents the sort of riverside landscape that I most enjoy. I have changed it from the actual place by slightly altering the course of the river, for reasons of composition, and by removing a fine Tudor house from the background, in order to make the picture show an environment rather than an identifiable piece of Hertfordshire scenery. As a boy, I found the lush, boot-squelching meadows so irresistible that my explorations were likely to end with me having soaking feet or even falling in the water. Now, I recognize these meadows as havens for wildlife – they are where you will find snipe in winter, where there are water voles, water shrews and such birds as moorhens, water rails and herons. The river that I have painted will certainly contain trout.

As it stands, it is a most attractive place. Although I am no expert on cattle, I am sure that the luxuriant vegetation and the rich variety of wild flowers are ideal for dairy cattle. Whatever their agricultural merits, though, the water meadows are important for the future survival of our wildlife. Every one of the largely undisturbed rough corners of the countryside is a nature reserve in its own right. Draining the water meadows may increase their productivity, but it does so at the expense of destroying them as natural habitats.

The same considerations apply to any established grassland, whether it is grazed directly, like the downs, or mown for hay. Over very many years, each sort of grassland develops its own characteristic collection of plant species, from the cuckoo flowers and kingcups of the water meadows to the wild thyme and orchids of the chalk downs. In Dorset, I can still find fields dotted with cowslips in the same profusion as daisies on a lawn. Essentially plants of old meadows, cowslips have declined in numbers as the meadows have been ploughed up or turned into nothing but grass factories. It is only now, when the yellow bunches of cowslip flowers have become an unusual and thrilling sight throughout much of England, that their disappearance

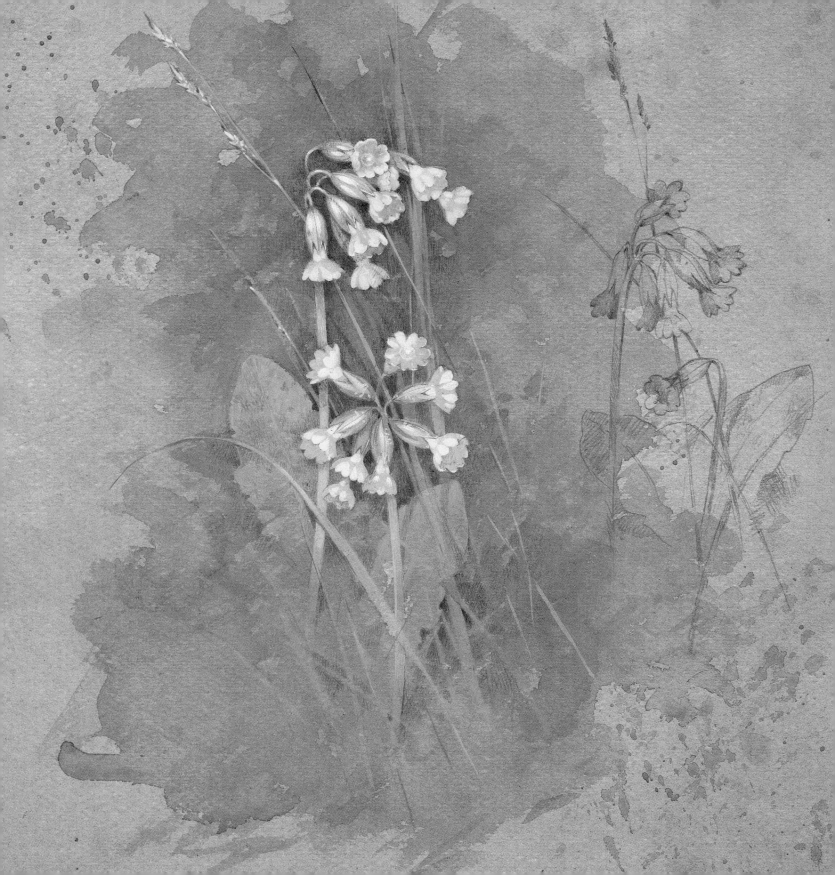

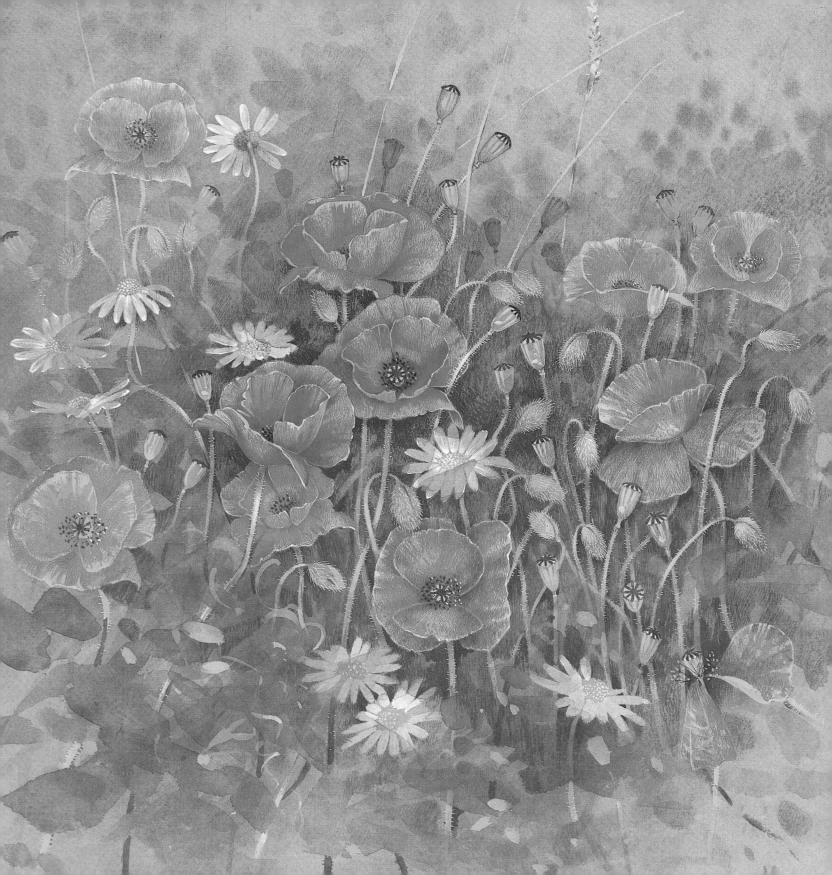

has really been noticed, and they have become something of a symbol of the countryside under threat.

Arable land, like grassland, once had its own range of wild flowers, among them poppies and others whose names show how they were identified with their habitat – cornflowers, corn cockles and corn marigolds. From the extent to which these have been eliminated, it looks as if their existence actually gave offence to a yield-conscious society. For my painting, I found a mass of poppies on a piece of arable land that was too small to be of much use. It seems that poppy seeds can lie dormant and safe from selective weedkillers so that they are still there to come up when the circumstances are favourable. Close by the field of poppies, in a secluded part of the Ashridge estate, there are still masses of primroses and violets in spring. It is a curious thought that it is now quite properly against the law for a passer-by to dig up wild flowers such as primroses, while the owner of the land would be perfectly within his rights to wipe them out with weedkillers.

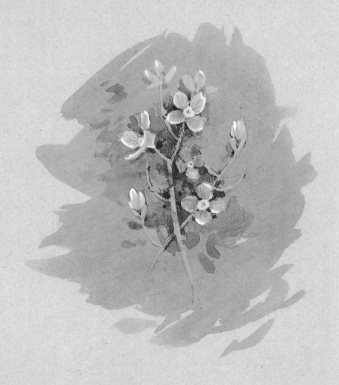

Fields today are four times the size that they were in my youth. In the immediate area, the estate has kept the relatively small fields with plenty of hedgerow and woodland, but, in the main, fields have become larger and larger in Hertfordshire, just as they have in most counties of southern England. The change has been produced by stripping out the hedges. Strangely, once the process of removal gets under way, it is not restricted to hedges between fields, but also extends to those round the edges of farms, beside lanes and roads, while others have fallen foul of road-widening schemes. I can see the crude economic sense in taking away hedgerows on arable land to produce the maximum uninterrupted acreage, but I cannot understand why landowners want to remove hedges on meadow land and replace them with barbed wire fences.

The remaining hedgerows are often brutally treated. There is a terrible machine called a flail, which is supposed to trim hedges but leaves them shattered. It will lay into quite large boughs which are overhanging and rip them away rather than sawing them off, sometimes tearing out great strips right back to the trunk. This is pure vandalism. A few years ago, any labourer who had been asked by his employer to cut the hedge and had treated it that way would have been instantly sacked.

I recently went to give a lecture on a nature reserve where the warden and his friends had spent a thousand hours or more laying a hedge properly. The adjoining land was rented to a local farmer, who went round this carefully laid hedge with a flail, sometimes cutting five feet into it. When the warden complained, the farmer said that he thought he was doing him a favour. The warden was so incensed that he took the matter to court.

It is said that you can tell the age of a hedgerow from the variety of plant species that it contains. The richest have taken scores, even hundreds of years to mature. A hedge that has been savaged with a flail can take years to recover; a hedge that has been ripped out will take more than a lifetime to replace properly, even if there was someone who would replant it. Something that has taken a century to develop can be destroyed with

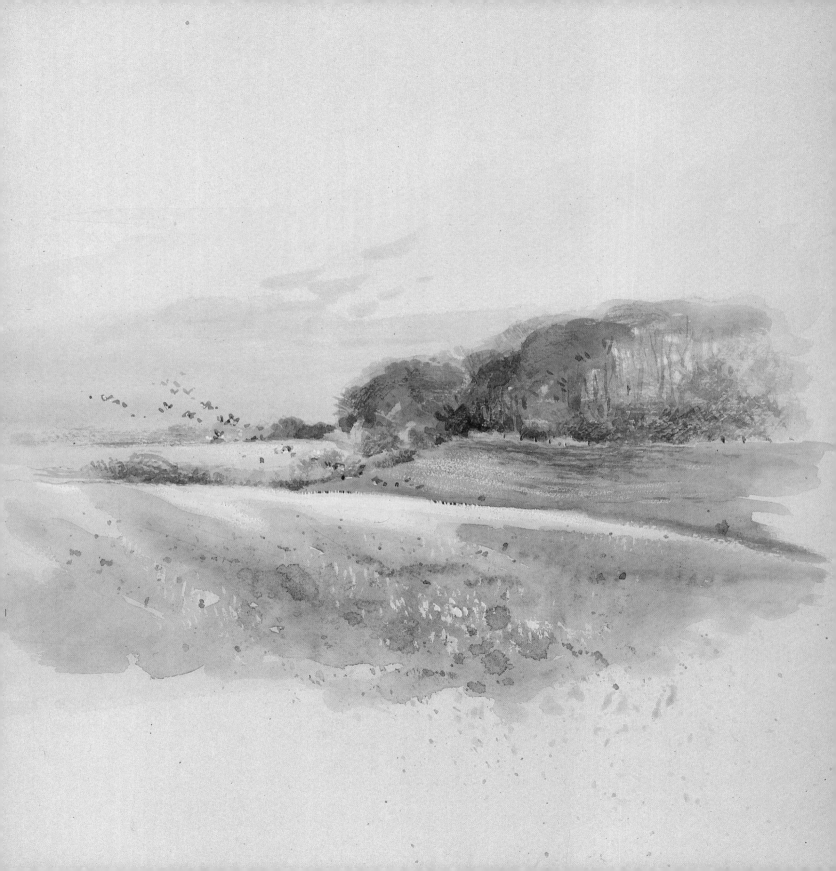

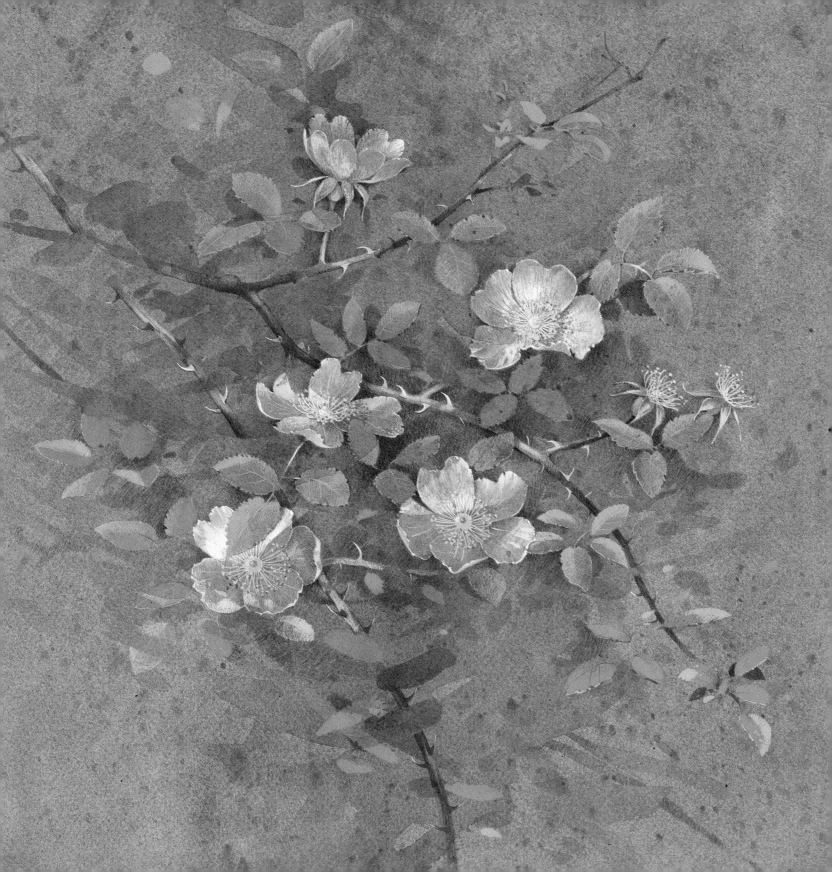

modern equipment in a couple of days – a poignant example of the vulnerability of the countryside.

It is the hedgerows that give the landscape of southern England much of its character. They contain many of its most characteristic plants and provide cover for its mammals, birds and insects. No cultivated rose for me can quite equal the wild roses of the hedgerows, which remind me of old ladies' flowery hats. Indeed, the more that garden roses are like wild ones, the more I like them. The big old hazel hedge in my garden provides my family with more nuts than we can use and attracts squirrels and great spotted woodpeckers. I have seen woodpeckers take a nut, wedge it into a crack in a tree and hammer at it like a nuthatch.

The countryside of hedgerows, copses and small woodlands has best survived the onslaught of modern agriculture on the great estates. Where the land belongs to some distant property company, there is little to protect it, but where the local landlord still lives on his estate, he may well have other interests than the financial return. Thus it is that sport has been of some importance in conservation. Whatever the landowner hunts or shoots, it requires the cover offered by woods and hedges if it is to maintain itself on the estate. As land completely devoid of cover would be the worst possible place for game, his interest in leaving the country as it is can outweigh the simple profit motive for rationalizing.

What is being preserved on a sporting estate is in effect the nature of the landscape. The danger is that the environment and the game are all that will be preserved. The key figure here is the gamekeeper, and the temptation is to get rid of any predators that would be likely to include the game in their diet. I believe that gamekeepers are very much better in this respect than they were, say, twenty years ago. Now that birds of prey are so low in numbers, any gamekeeper who shoots one deserves to be dealt with severely. In fact, the whole practice of shooting vermin – which includes anything that might prey on the game birds, from stoats and weasels to crows – is one countryside tradition that I would be glad to see dying out.

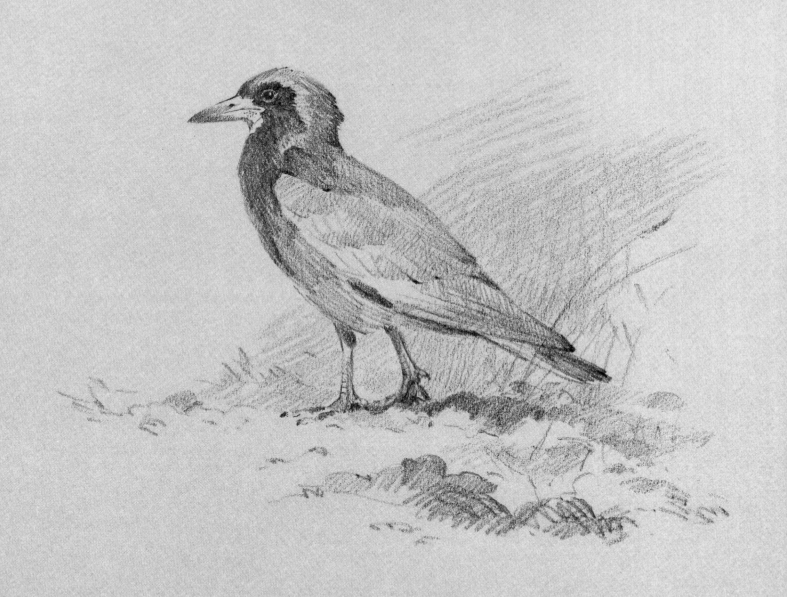

We should not imagine, though, that it is the gamekeepers who have destroyed our wildlife – far greater forces have been at work.

A major part of many gamekeepers' jobs is to stock the land with game. If the predators take some of it, the response should not be to go after them with a gun, but to feel honoured to have helped provide for them. In the same way, if you stock a river with trout, you should expect the herons to come down and take a few. I am against any sporting interest that involves attacking the predators to any extent. If the fisherman sees a heron floating away at dawn when he is thinking of going down and casting a fly over the river, he should just tip his hat to it and say, 'Good luck to you. You were there before me.' It is just as wrong to be violently greedy in this

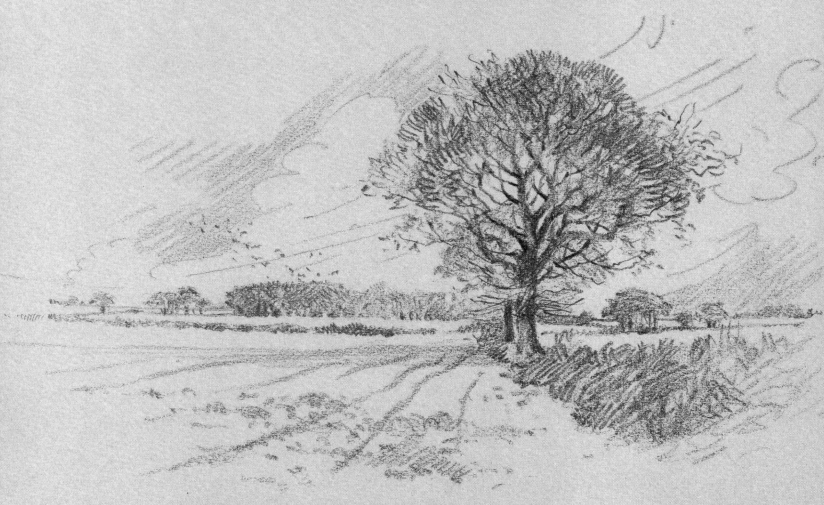

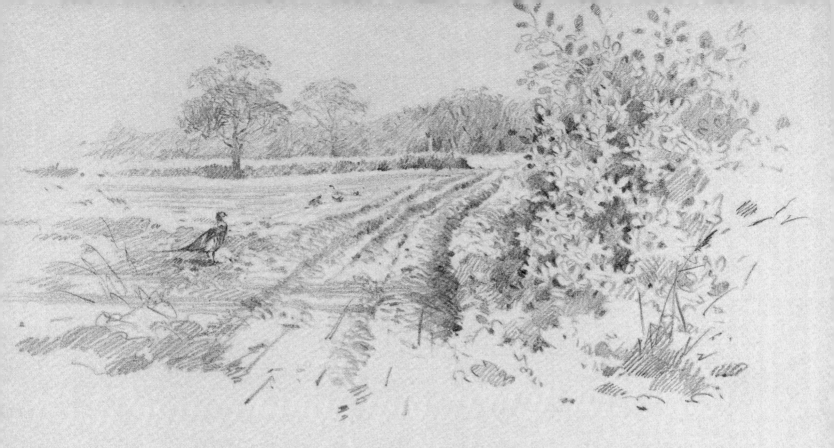

respect as it is to hack out the hedgerows. In our management of the countryside, we need to live at one with nature, to stop thinking that we are superior beings. Humans, after all, are predators on the largest scale that the world has ever known.

The most unpleasant aspect of man the predator is not his hunting activities but what he is willing to do to obtain his meat: the horrors of factory farming and of calves, pigs and chickens living out their entire existence without seeing the light of day. The awful counterpart of using the land for intensive crop production is tidying the animals away into buildings designed for maximum output with minimum effort. In the traditional pattern of mixed farming, animal husbandry and crop-raising went hand in hand, with each contributing to the other, and the countryside had a unity about it that is more and more being undermined by the policy of using technology to wring the last ounce of production out of the land.

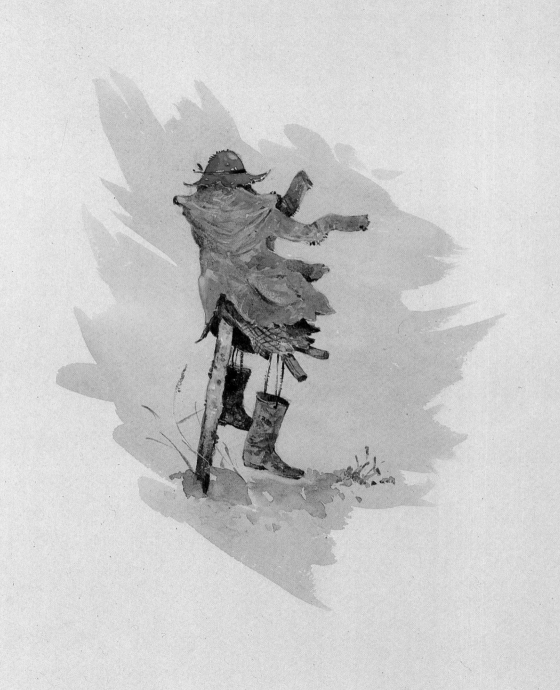

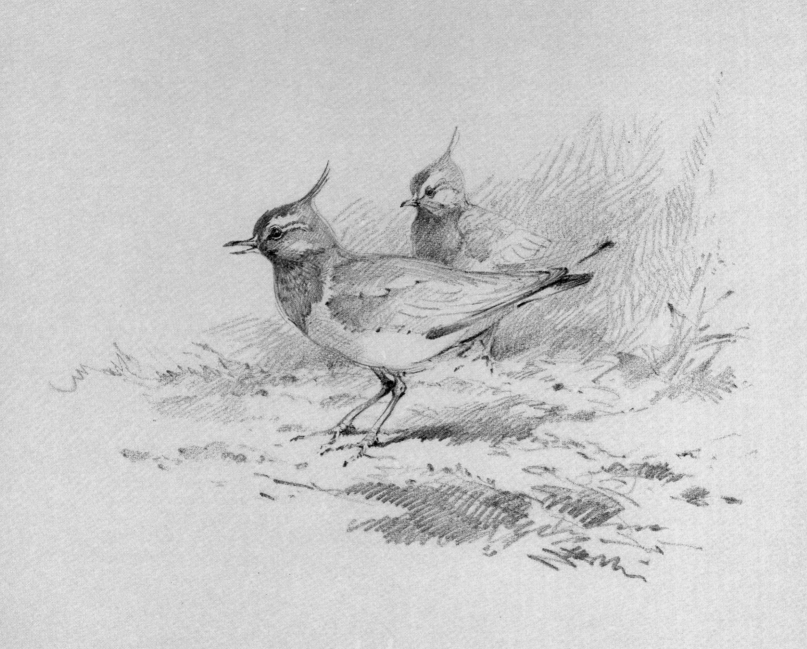

No wonder, then, that I derive such pleasure from the sight of farm animals in their natural surroundings: dairy cows chewing the cud in the lush water meadows, sheep scattered across the windy expanses of the South Downs. I have chosen to end this chapter with pictures of pigs because they are now so often reared in indoor piggeries, and it is particularly pleasing to see them out in the fields where they belong. There is nothing particularly special about them – they are just local free-range pigs. The ones in the large painting are thoroughly enjoying themselves sloshing around in the muddy corner of a field in autumn, rooting for their food and eating the acorns that have fallen to the ground under the oak trees in the hedgerows. As I looked at them, the one in the foreground peered up at me, and her ear swung back as she lifted her head. Anyone who thinks of pigs as gross, sleepy creatures in sties will be surprised at just how active and lively free-range ones can be. The piglets I have painted rushing out of an old barn were making a tremendous noise and generally expressing joy at being out and about. This, for me, is how pigs should be.

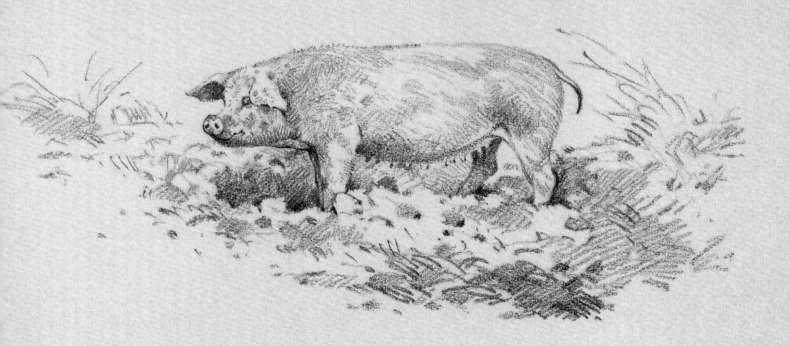

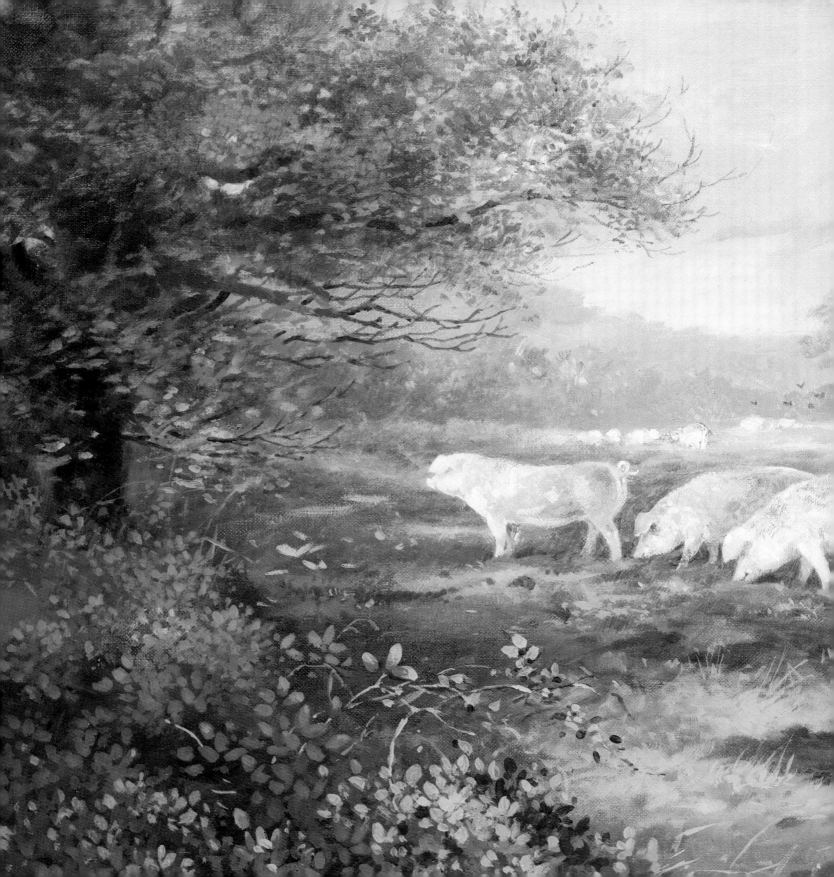

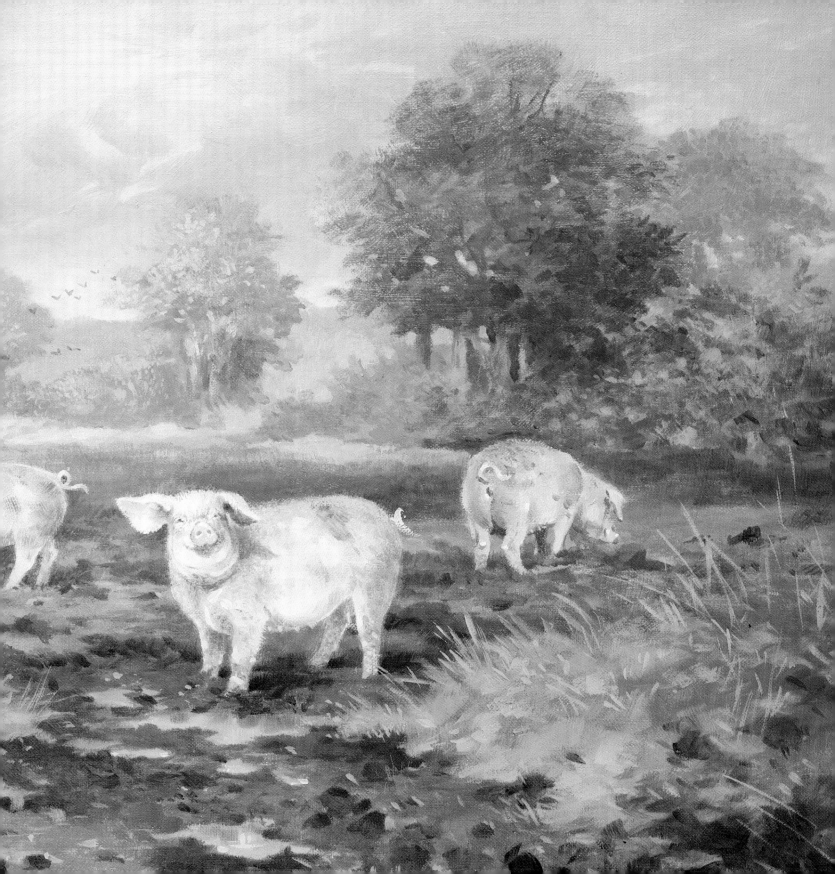

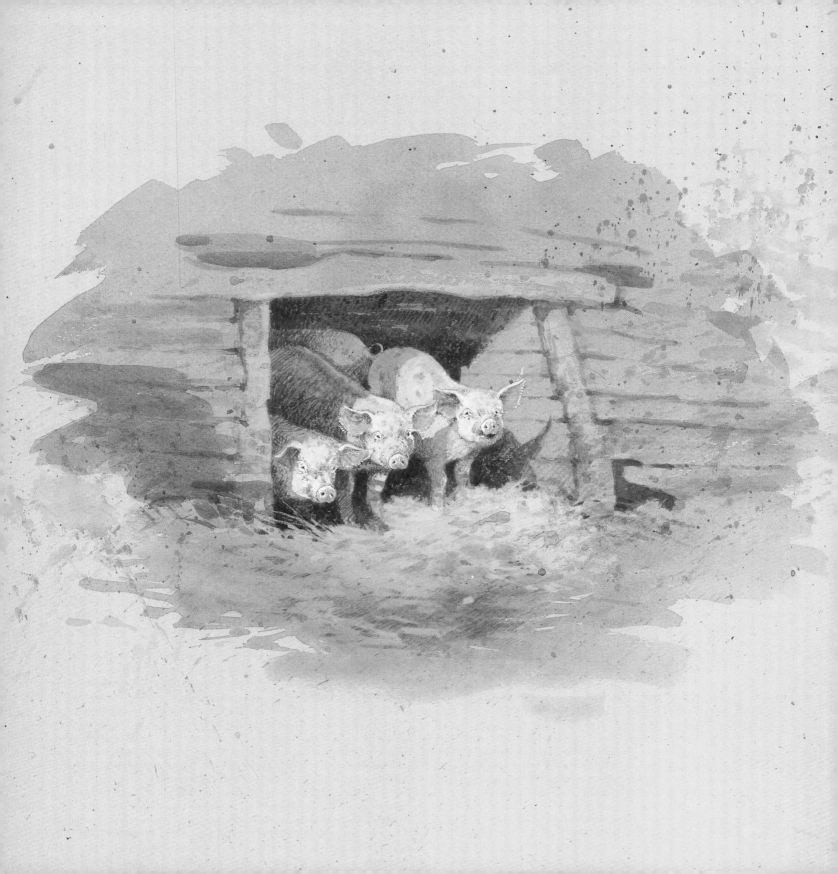

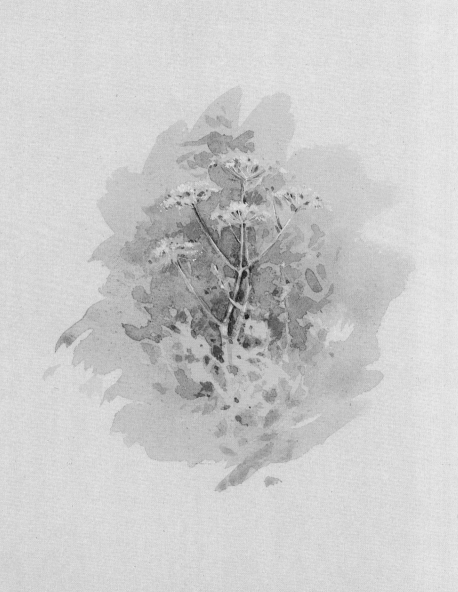

Carts, Gates and Barns

As I was brought up to be a craftsman and to work with craftsmen, anything made by hand from natural materials has a fascination for me. I can think of no more superb example than the work of a wheelwright who manages to produce a functional vehicle that, at the same time, has great beauty. The wagon which I was lucky enough to find locally is of the sort that I most wanted to have: it is an Oxfordshire (or Woodstock) wagon which was actually built by Cannon & Son of Quainton in Buckinghamshire in 1907. It is a fairly large vehicle – a real harvest wagon – with a rather exaggerated but very elegant shape and fine craftsmanship. The spindle sides sweep up, front and back, and there are outvanes that hang out over the sides to take the overhang of a load of hay, corn or beet, and to stop straw falling on the wheels and clogging them up. These rays are functional attachments, but they are beautifully designed and made.

The wagon is fairly heavy, but could have been pulled by a big Shire horse, although for large loads a pair of horses with a pole between them might have been needed. It would have been used mainly around the farm at harvest and hay time. Because it was the largest sort of wagon, it would have been the one that was loaded up for making hay ricks. A wagon like this would also have been used for communal outings such as Sunday School trips: the village children would decorate the vehicle and put flowers around the horse's ears before they all piled in and set off.

Now the wheels are a little shaky and the floor will need to be replaced, but the basic structure is still very sound in view of the fact that the wagon has stood out in the open for many years. I shall need some help in restoring it, although I have no desire to put it back into a pristine condition. It is still movable even now – after all, it will never need to go round the fields again. It would be only too easy to put in replacement parts, but taking away the original material would remove some of the cart's great charm. Wherever I can, I shall fill the existing wood and impregnate it with resin

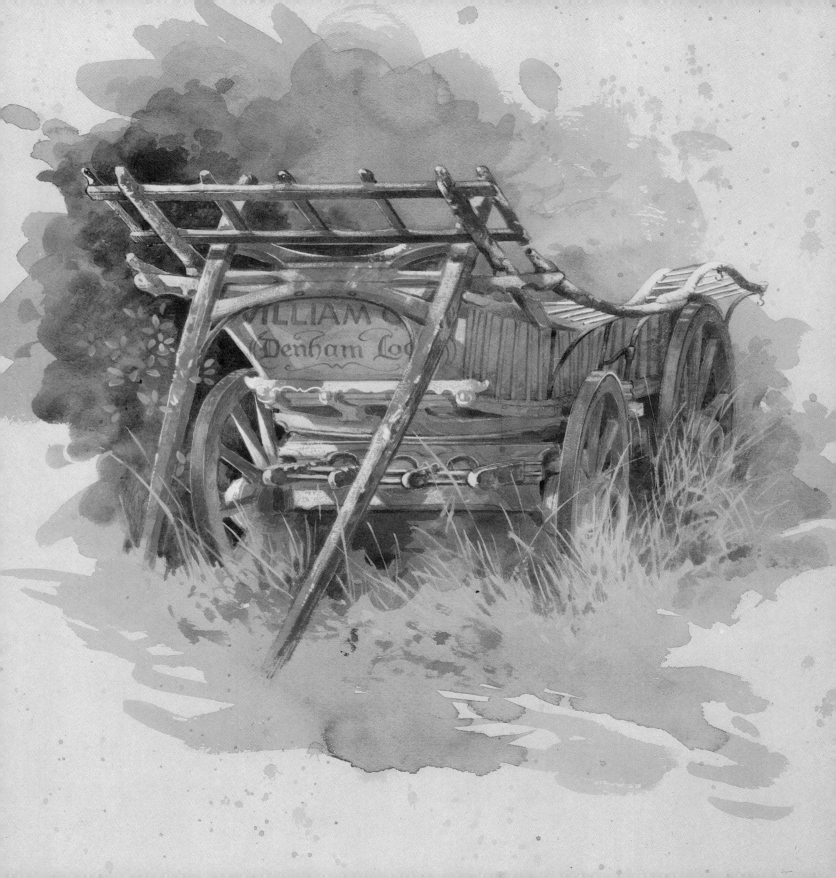

to preserve it. The value of the wagon for me is in its associations, which are functional: it was built to do a job of work, and that is what excites my imagination.

Other man-made things I have always loved in the countryside are wooden gates and stiles, from five-bar farmyard gates made of oak, like the one I have at the entrance to my garden, down to primitive stiles which use any piece of wood that happens to be handy. These things are simple and unaffected; their natural materials fit into the countryside in a way that barbed wire entanglements never can.

Stiles and open gateways have a beckoning quality, which makes me want to approach, to climb over the stile or go through the gate, because beyond there may be undreamed-of sights to be seen. Particularly when the sun is shining and I can glimpse a field on the other side, I can imagine a fantasy

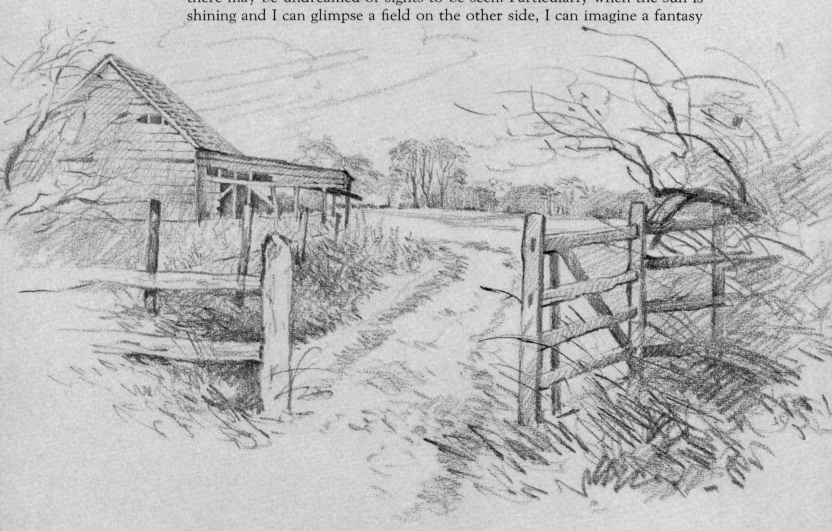

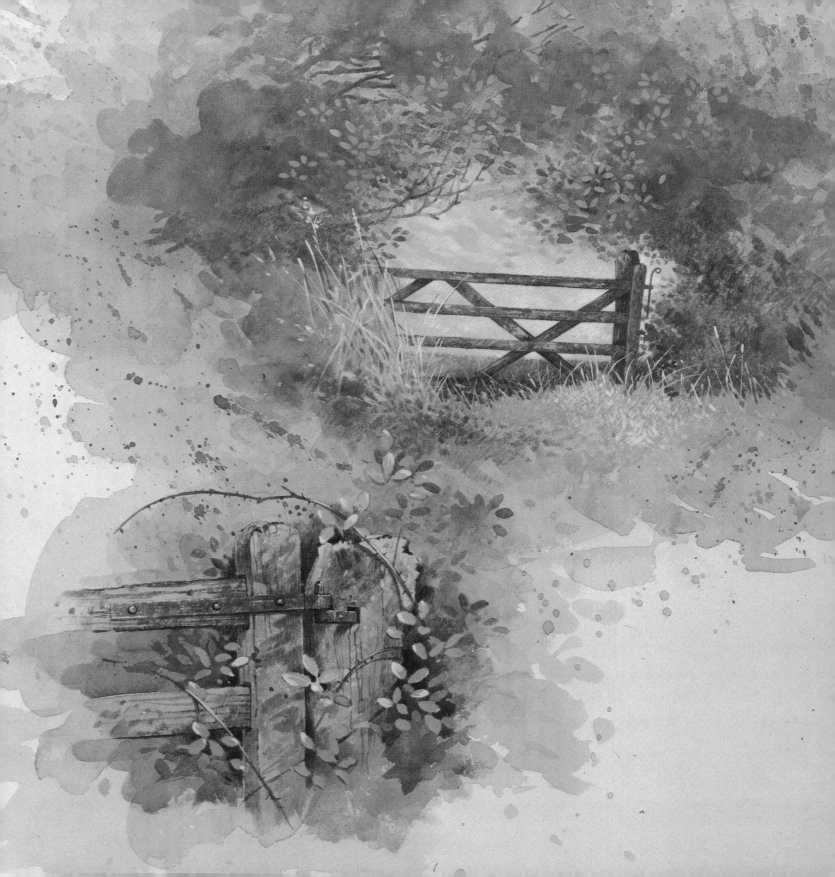

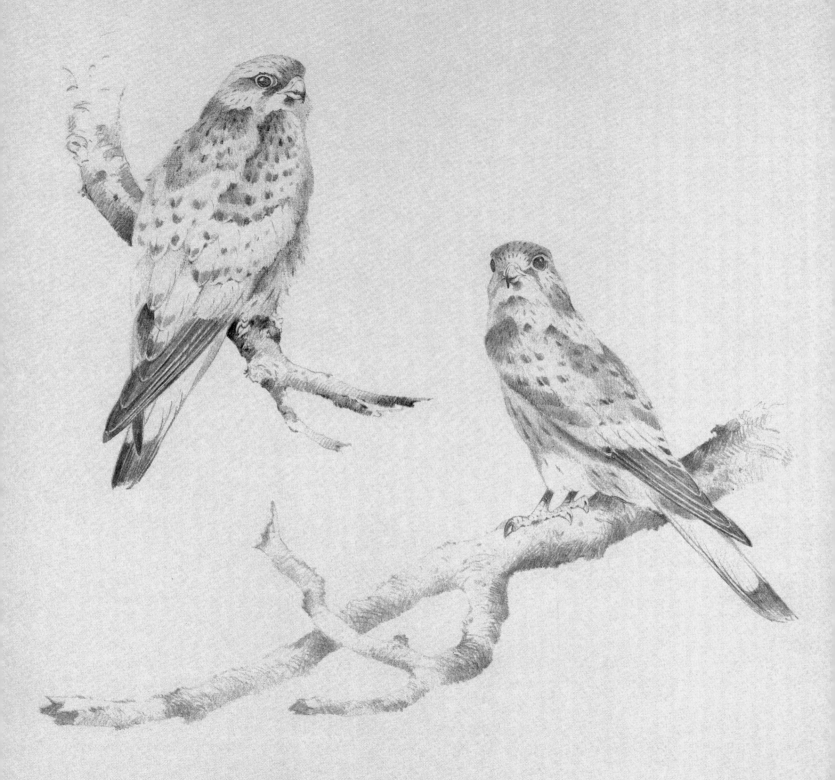

world that could be out there. And when you do go through, if you are very careful and just peep round the hedgerow, you will very often see mammals and birds for a fleeting moment before they see you. In my drawing of kestrels, I have shown one which I was able to observe through binoculars without his seeing me. He was totally relaxed, with his feathers loose and puffed up, so that he looked fat and comfortable. Then he was alarmed by noticing me. All his feathers lay down and he was streamlined – in a few seconds he would be off. The picture came out of the contrast in the bird's shape before and after he had seen me. My favourite countryside offers such chances for hiding that even humans have a chance of catching animals unawares.

The small gate with a rose arch that I have painted is based on one that I have rebuilt in my garden. Rustic arches like this are typical of old-

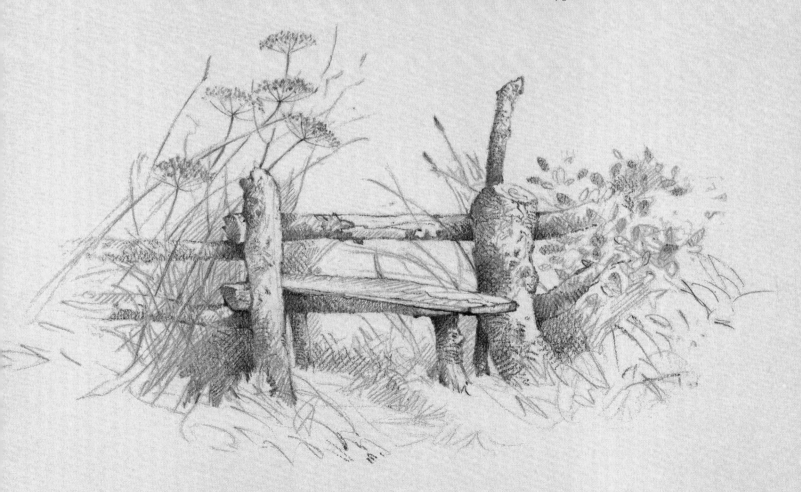

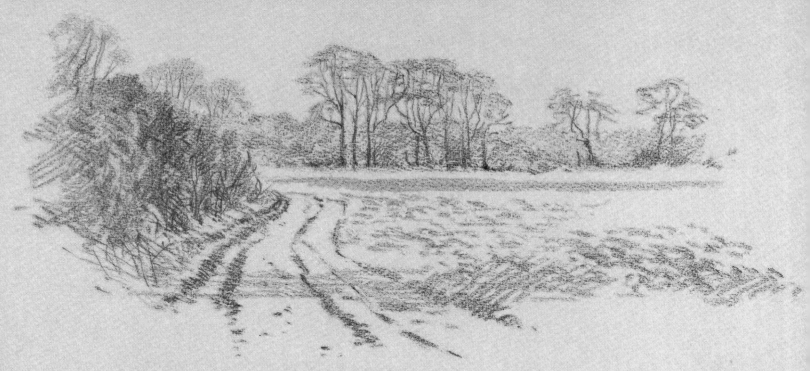

fashioned cottage gardens and are not too sophisticated to have the same effect on me as gateways in hedgerows. They are inviting, possibly hiding something mysterious; they are part of the way that the countryside seems to draw me into it. Lanes and tracks, perhaps curving off out of sight, are no less magnetic – they make me want to walk down them to find out what is around the next corner. In my pictures, tracks that have been heavily rutted by wheels express some of this feeling by drawing the eye into the picture.

The five-bar gates that traditionally went with tracks like these have often been allowed to decay and eventually have been replaced by tubular metal objects which at best are only inconspicuous. Even that virtue is not usually shared by the prefabricated concrete and asbestos structures that are to-day's farm buildings. Old barns are often buildings of great beauty, but they are unfortunately not very convenient, now that agriculture relies so much on heavy machinery.

The medieval barn I have drawn is a sad reminder of the difficulties that face the conservation of rural England. It was said to be one of the oldest

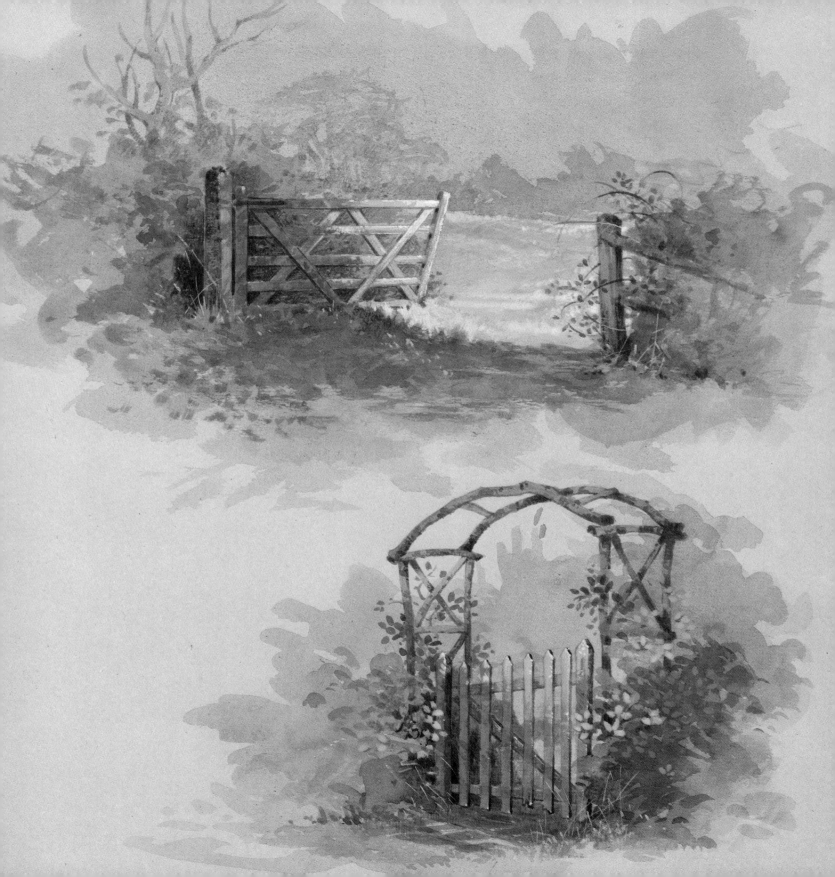

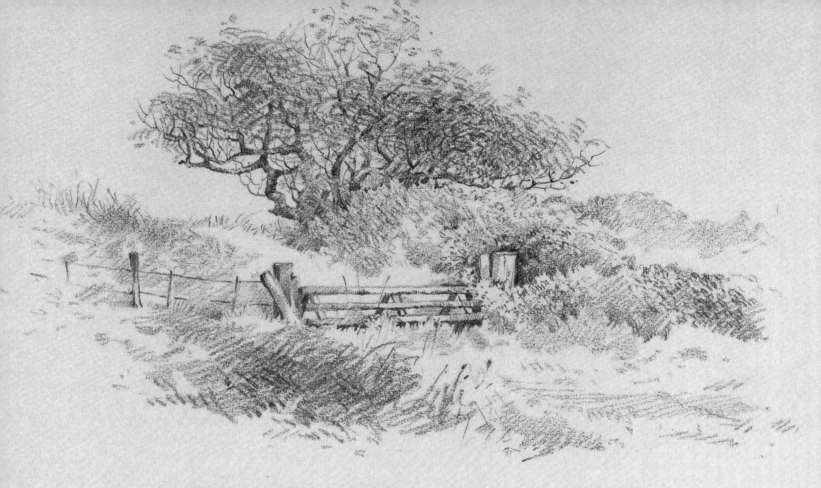

barns in the south and was of cruck construction, like a boat upside down –
one of the earliest methods of building in timber. This Hertfordshire barn
was one of a cluster which together made up a rare surviving example of
the typical barnyard. The others were also attractive, though not as unusual
as this one, but the whole group was well worth saving. Its disappearance
illustrates the inadequacy of preservation procedures.

For some years, I had been involved in efforts to preserve this barn,
which certainly needed some repair work. Nothing much happened in
response to these efforts until one day I was asked to have a look at the
building, as a large hole had appeared in it. When I got there, I was
astonished to find that the barn had fallen down almost completely after
having stood for hundreds of years.

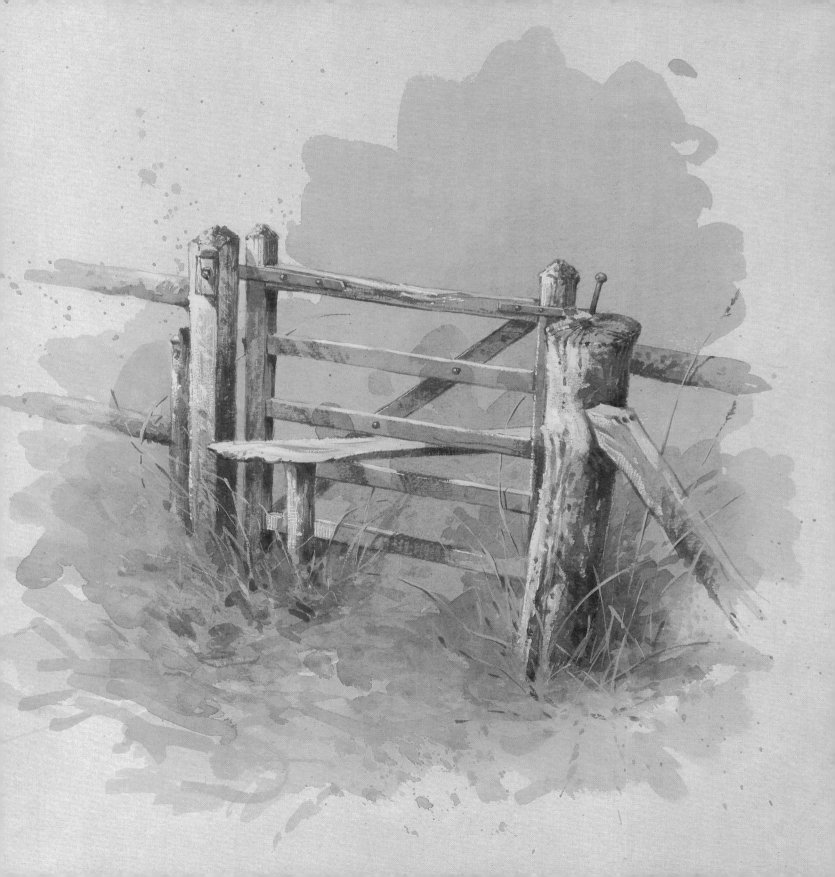

In my view, anyone who owns a building like this has an obligation to look after it – I cannot understand why anybody would want to buy such very old property and let it fall into disrepair. Yet when this happens, preservation orders seem to be of little use. In this case, I know that grants were available for its repair and voluntary organizations were prepared to do the work for nothing.

At the moment, though much may happen in the few months before this book is published, the barn has been reduced to a pile of numbered pieces of wood so that it can be put together again. There are offers to rebuild it in an open-air museum and on a nearby estate, and it is possible that it may be re-erected on its original site. In any case, though, it is sad that the barn has to stop being a functional farm building and turn into a museum piece.

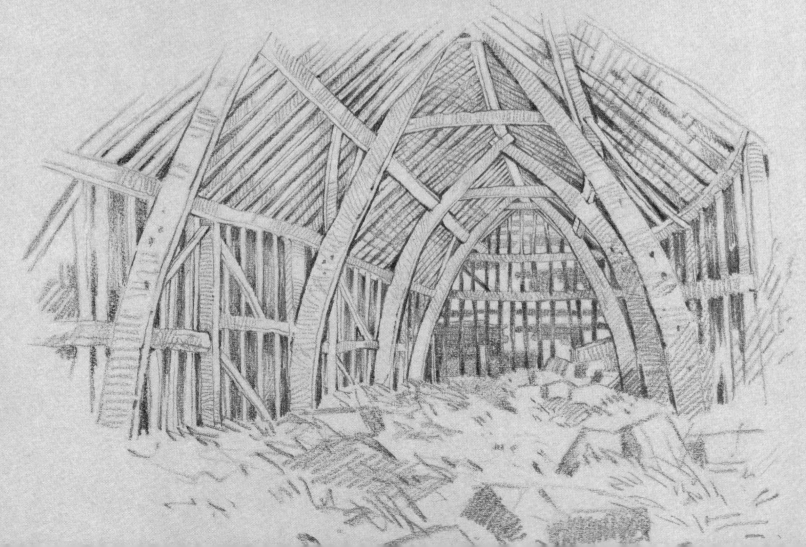

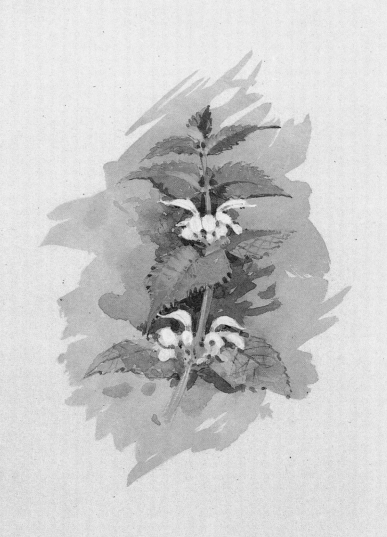

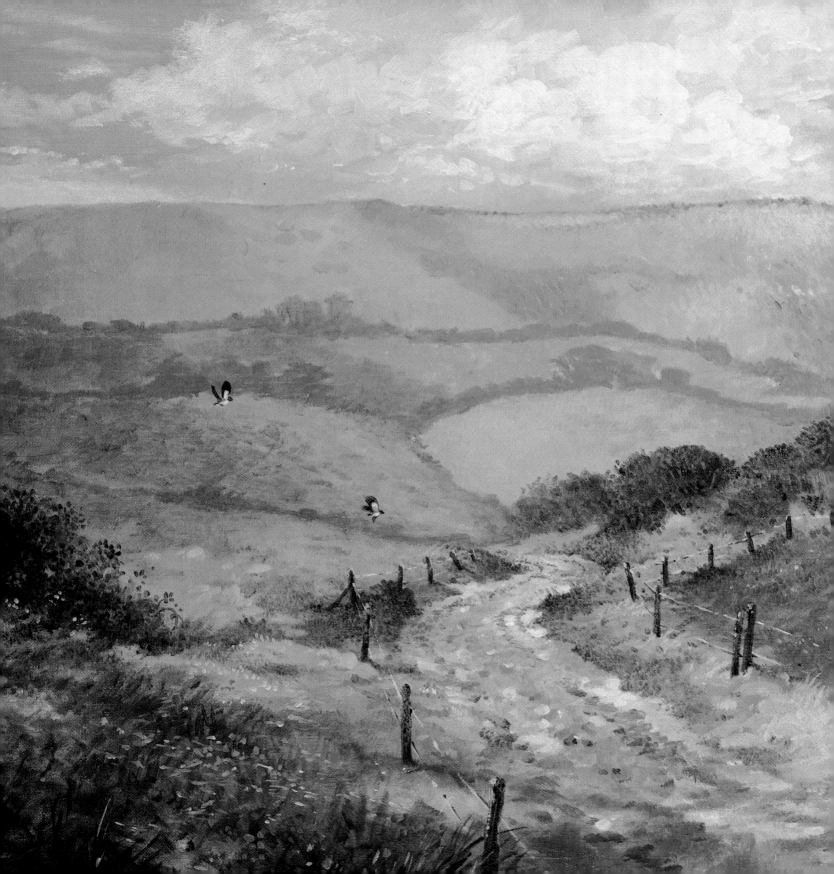

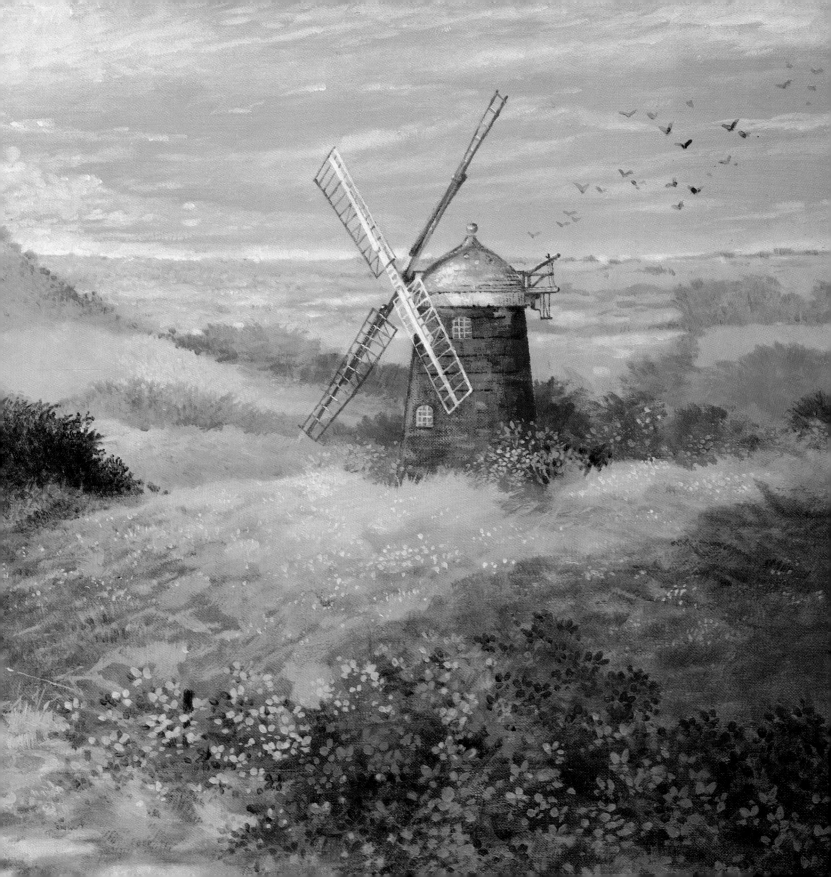

Downs

The downs could hardly be more different from the enclosed countryside of hedgerows and woodlands: they are airy and fresh, with beautiful, spacious skylines. Birds lift off from the turf and are swept away by the wind. Because the downs are so wild and open, they give as great a feeling of remoteness as you can get in southern England: I feel that my imagination is free to roam, and I find myself thinking about the shepherds of the past and the days when great tracts of the South Downs were grazed by sheep.

Even now, there are sheep on parts of the downland. The best time of the year for me is during spring lambing. I also love the downs in the late summer, when it can often be very hot and I can find two of my favourite butterflies, the adonis blue, which is rather rare, and the chalkhill blue, which also occurs on the Chiltern Hills, a few miles north of my cottage.

I go to Dorset to see the downs as they have been for centuries. There, the turf extends right to the edge of the cliffs and is part of a coastline that is very keenly preserved. This is a very ancient countryside, full of relics of the Iron Age and its settlements – inland there are remote Iron Age fortresses on the hills. The particular joy here is the deep, springy carpet of turf, which has been closely cropped since time immemorial by sheep and rabbits, so that it has developed its own special flora and insect life. It contains the wild thyme on which the large blues used to live and masses of other wild flowers such as harebells and eyebrights and orchids.

This unique environment has vanished from great stretches of the Sussex downs, which were ploughed up so that more crops could be grown. As it took centuries for the turf to develop, it can never be recreated. The ploughed areas of the Sussex downs are now rather desolate and lifeless stretches of prairie.

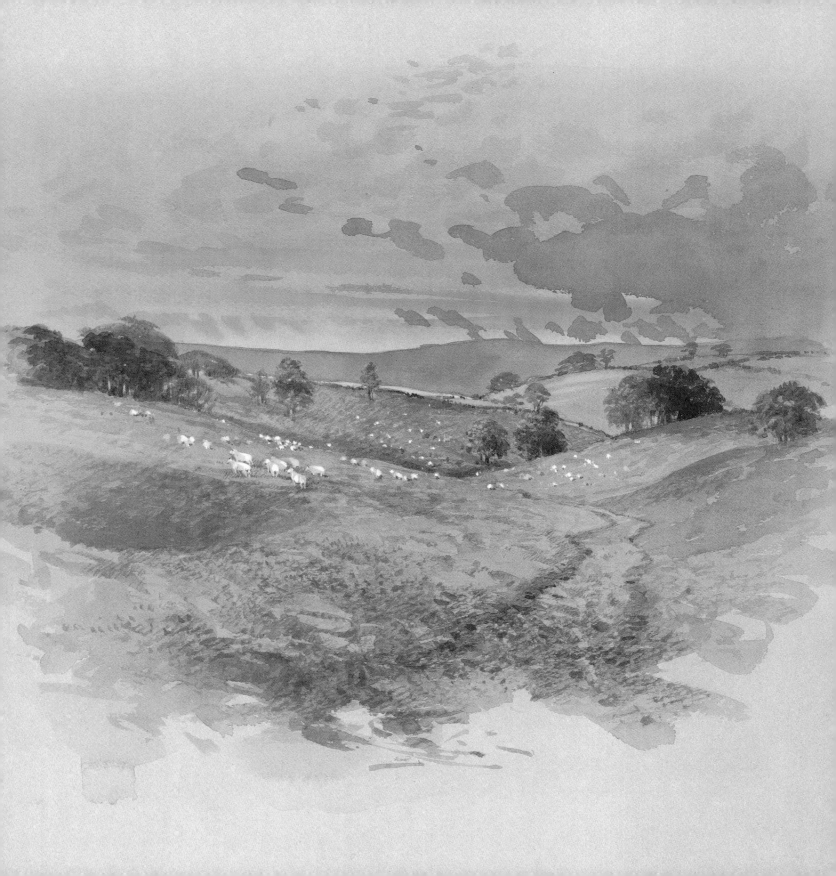

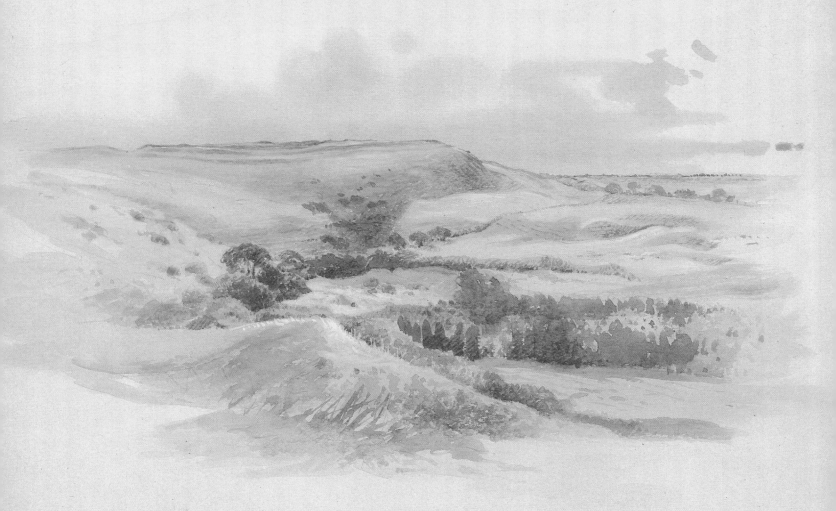

My large picture with a windmill is inspired by the South Downs in Sussex, a county that I am just beginning to discover. Apart from a brief stay there with my parents during the war, I did not know it at all until my interest in shepherds led me back there. The picture is not an exact record of the particular place, which actually had two windmills. As there was more ploughing than I wanted to show, I have restored some of the turf.

When I think of the downlands of today, I think of skylarks and of the scrubby blackthorn and hawthorn which have often taken over in areas where the rabbit population was decimated by myxomatosis and the turf

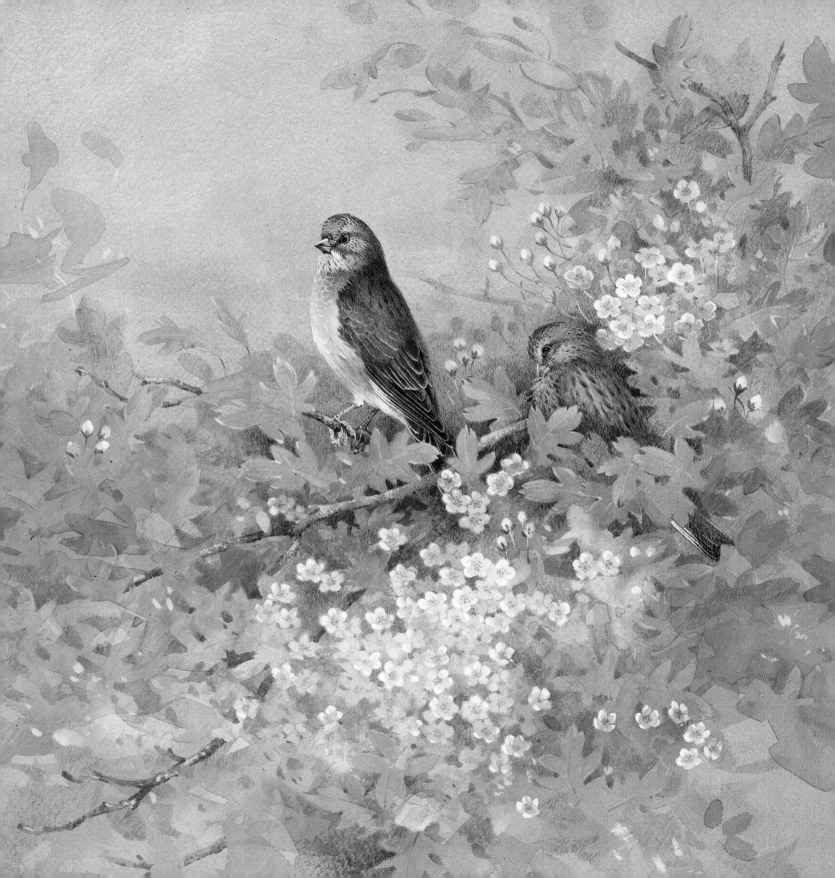

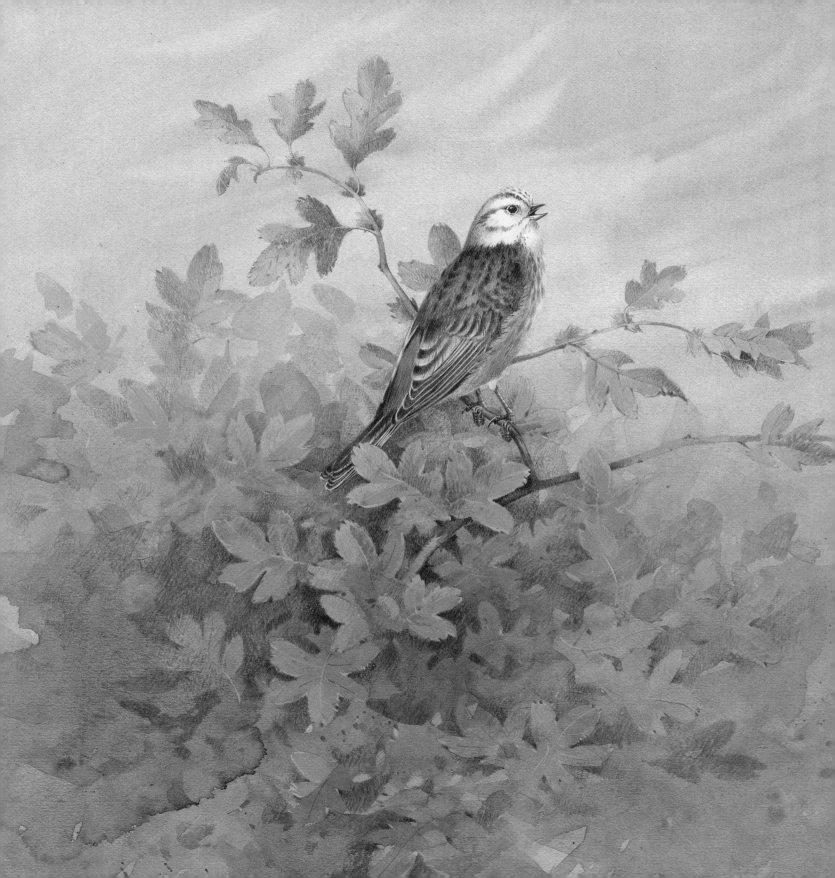

was less intensively grazed by sheep alone. Now a characteristic sight is a
yellowhammer singing from the topmost branch of a hawthorn with his
head showing a dazzling yellow in the sunlight; the scrubby chalk downs of
the Chilterns are a habitat for small songbirds such as linnets and warblers,
while many of the flowers that used to thrive on the open downs have been
lost. Both the linnets and the yellowhammer have been painted as you will
see them on the Chilterns; the linnet is shown in late spring, surrounded
with hawthorn blossom.

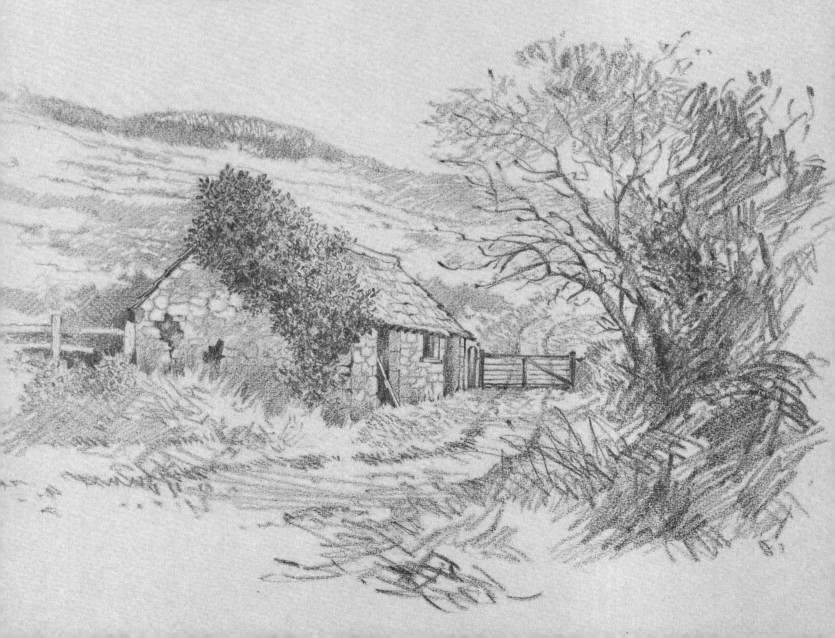

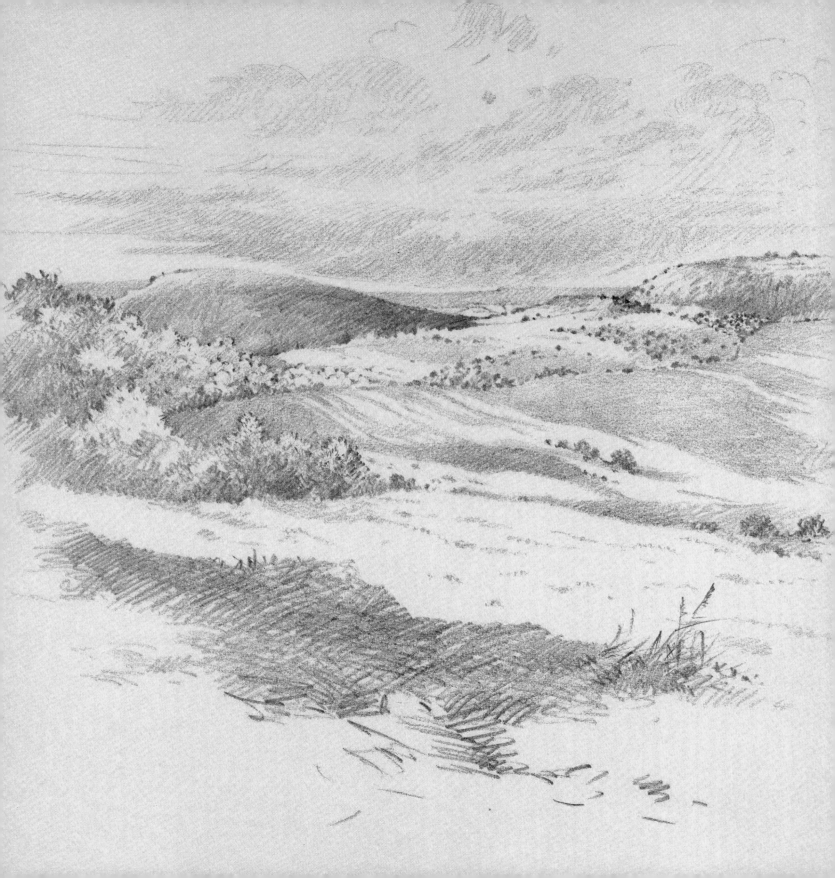

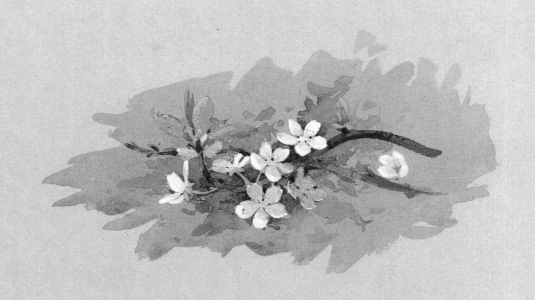

The Shepherd

Many years ago, a friend who is an antique dealer gave me a shepherd's chair. It is a rather enclosed wooden armchair which perhaps used to protect the shepherd when he sat out all night in his hut during lambing.

The associations that the chair had for me were with Gabriel Oak and his hut on Norcombe Hill in Thomas Hardy's *Far from the Madding Crowd*. I have always been fascinated by Hardy, and my interest in shepherds has developed over the years to the point where I have searched for shepherds' crooks and sheep bells – I now have quite a collection of them.

The shepherds of southern England had their own traditional equipment and their own way of working, which suited the countryside. Until the Second World War, particularly in the South Downs area of Sussex, they were still using the Old English sheepdog, a long-haired, hardy breed that was much more of a guard dog than many of its modern counterparts. Now it has become a show animal because most of the shepherds who used it have disappeared, and the usual sheepdog is the collie.

After his dog, the shepherd's next most important possession is his crook, which is almost a badge of office. Where northern crooks were all of wood or had a ram's-horn head, the southern ones were of iron with

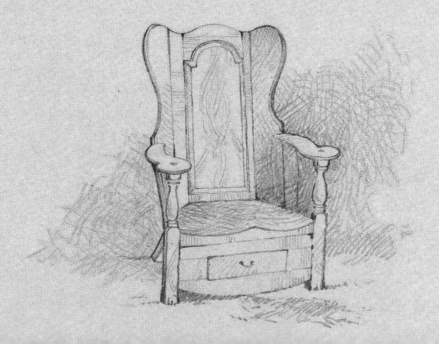

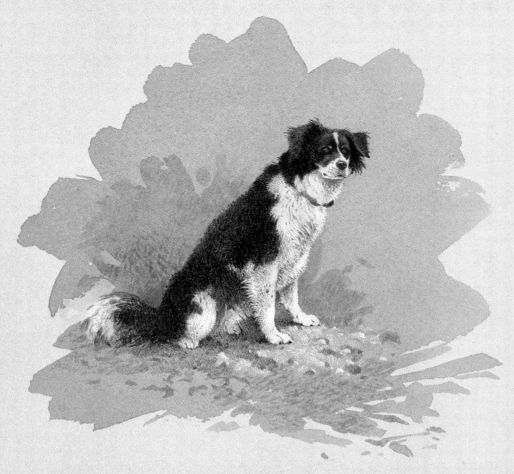

wooden stems, usually made by a blacksmith in the village, often to the shepherd's own requirements, although there are certain recognizable patterns, for example in Sussex. The iron crooks were handed down from father to son and lasted for generations.

I look upon traditional shepherds as people apart, because there are hardly any of them left and because of their associations for me. Surprisingly, just a few miles up the road from my cottage there is a shepherd, a very traditional one, called Alan Lungley. I was walking along one evening in the winter with a friend, when I saw a lamp shining out from a hut in the middle of a field. We went towards the light and found Alan sitting on the steps of his hut with the ewes bedded down around him.

131

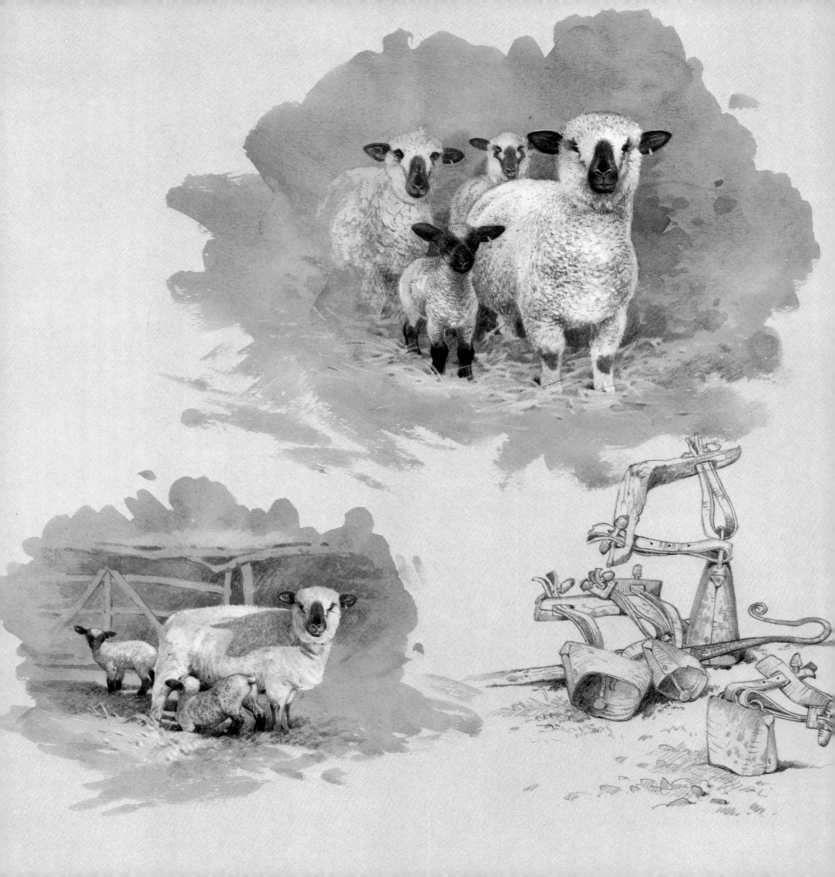

Alan is a storybook character – he believes in the techniques of the old shepherds and uses the old implements. He still puts bells on his sheep. The ones he uses are very old, probably Victorian, and came down to him from the previous shepherd on the farm. Like the ones I have drawn, they are cluckets, which are widest at the mouth and taper up to a narrow top with loops to take the leathers – normally bits of old harness that the shepherd has been able to find. The canister bell, which was apparently the favourite in Sussex, was straight-sided. Both varieties were made of sheet metal, folded and riveted into shape and coated in brass, which eventually wore off. The leathers were attached with wooden or bone lockers to a wooden yoke that was carved by the shepherd himself.

In the 'twenties, Barclay Wills wrote three books about the shepherds of Sussex and the South Downs. He bemoaned their disappearance and said that sheep bells were becoming quite rare. Yet fifty or so years later, I can still find a shepherd just up the lane who is working in the traditional way.

To look after sheep like that, you need to be tough and absolutely dedicated, and probably to have grown up in the job. Alan's father was a shepherd, and so was his grandfather – he comes from a line of top men in his profession. I believe that he moved from Suffolk about twenty years ago, when there were no more sheep in his area. The farm where he now works has always had good sheep and a traditional shepherd; Alan came when the previous one retired. As his knowledge of sheep is so great, he is left to himself and is effectively his own boss.

Unlike so many people today, Alan has not lost the joy of his work. Material things mean very little to him. His attitude to life is certainly not for everyone, but for total contentment and job satisfaction quite aside from monetary reward, we could well look at the shepherd. If you read about the countryside of fifty or more years ago, you can see that shepherds have always been like that. Alan is exactly the right type for the job: he is physically strong but very gentle, and as good with his dog as he is with his sheep.

Each year, during lambing, Alan lives out in his hut for two months – December and January. He builds a lambing yard out of timber and thatches it with straw. It presents an amazing picture, like stepping back into the last century. Inevitably, this sight and Alan's whole way of life combined with my interest in Samuel Palmer and Thomas Hardy to spark my imagination to the extent that there are few days when I do not find myself thinking about shepherds. Indeed, in a way, my whole involvement with the country-side and the people who work in it is crystallized in my fascination with the shepherd's way of life.

Although Alan works in the old ways, in many respects he has a modern approach – not that I, as an artist, am really aware of it. I look upon him as a romantic figure, although I am sure that if I suggested this to him, he would laugh in my face. He sees himself as just a man who works with sheep, but to me he is a subject, a part of the British countryside of the past yet, extraordinarily, also very much of today.

The sheep he rears are Hampshire Downs, and farmers come from all over the world to buy. Many people around here will tell you Alan has the very finest sheep because he is so completely devoted that he is willing to lie out with them all night at the worst time of year.

I have found him working in a barn with hand clippers, trimming around the sheeps' eyes and noses to prepare them. This method of working, I am told, is unusual these days, and Alan is one of the very few shepherds around here who know how to do it. What is important is that he does this, not to be theatrical, but because he has always done it, and done it very well. It is this traditional approach to a skill that fascinates me as an artist and reflects back to Thomas Hardy's portrait of Gabriel Oak. The romantic thing about Alan is that he knows nothing of all that; he is innocently working away and doing, by any standards, a magnificent job. I shall prob-ably never meet a man like that again, because it will be virtually impossible to replace him when he goes.

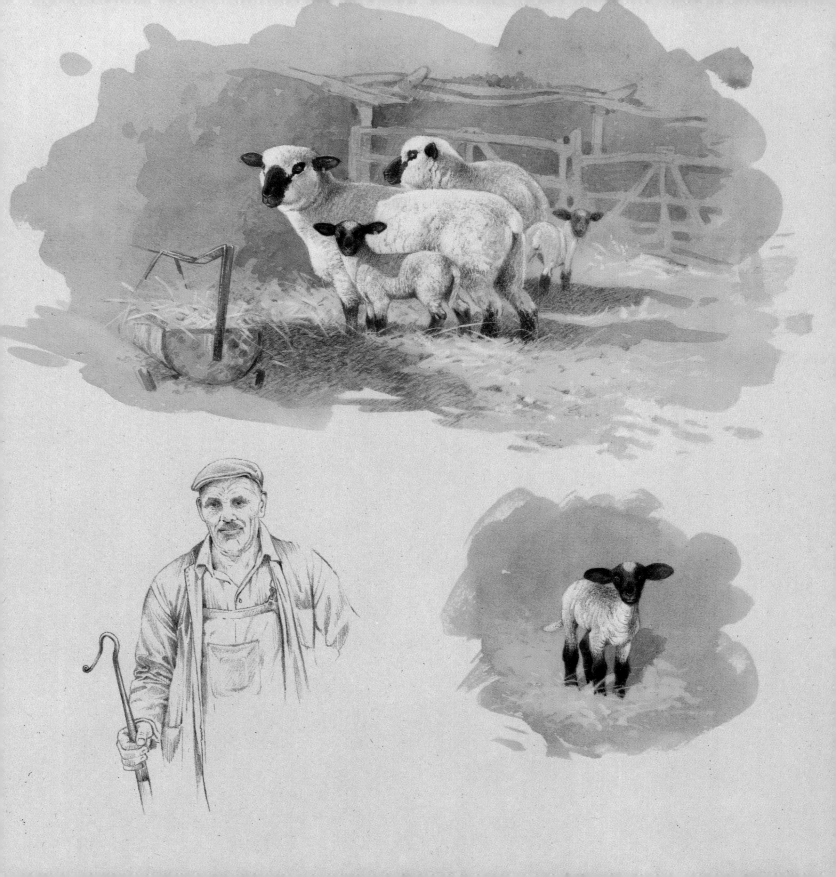

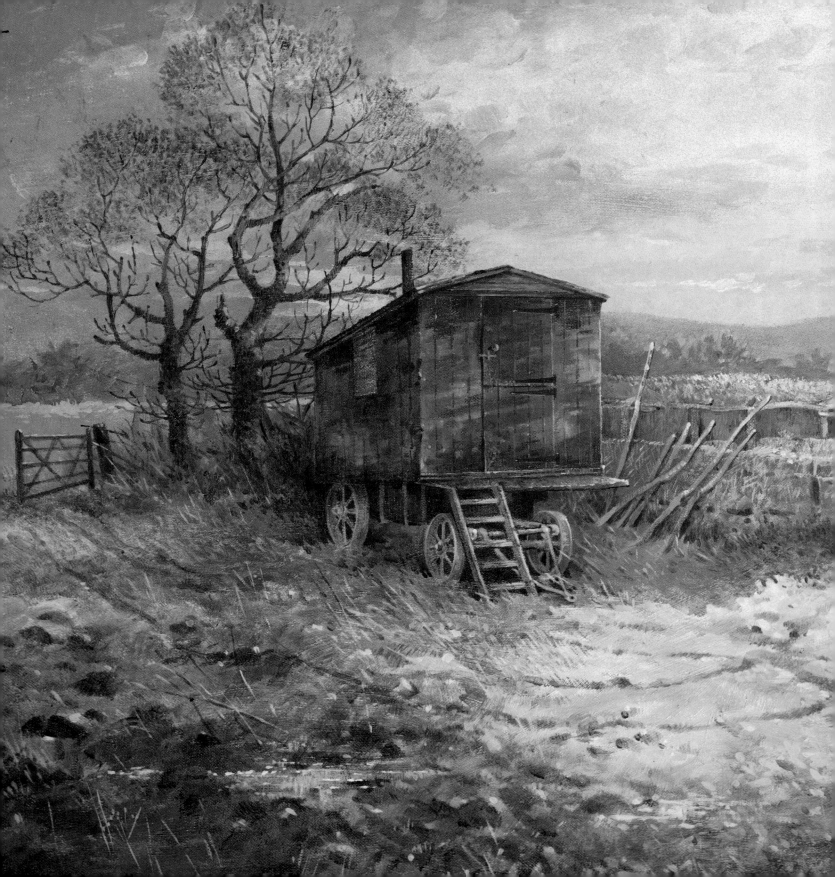

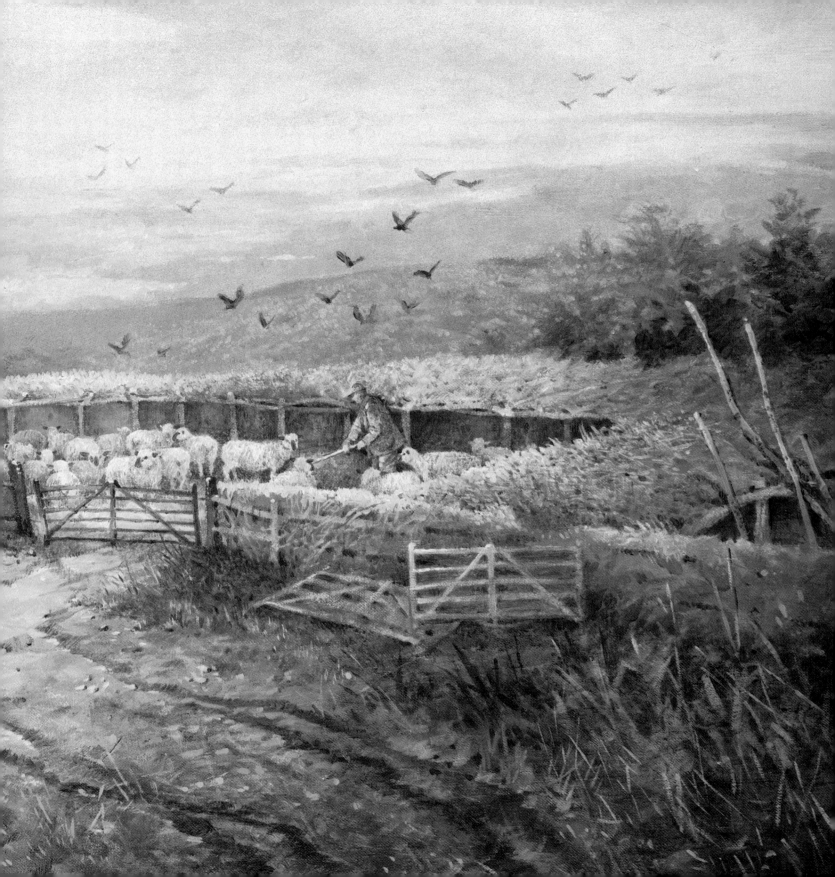

Epilogue

As you have seen, my countryside is not the England of moors, rocks and dry stone walls, but an altogether more gentle place of hedgerows, meadows and woodlands. Outsiders might find it unspectacular, perhaps dull, compared with the dramatic scenery that they can find elsewhere. But to me, it is inexhaustibly exciting, increasingly so as I continue to learn about it.

Yet even as I learn and become ever more immersed, I can feel it being destroyed all around me. It is in the heavily populated South of England that the threat is worst, not just from agriculture but from road building, gravel digging and urban sprawl. I cannot bear to contemplate the logical conclusion: a landscape containing only crops and people. The process of change is unlikely to halt of its own accord, because the cry is always for increased food production, although overeating is one of modern society's most serious health problems.

The question we have to ask ourselves is what we want the countryside to be. For the farmers, it is a source of livelihood,, but that should not exclude conservation. For many people, it is a source of pleasure or recreation, but catering too much for their interests would produce something between a safari park, an adventure playground and an open-air museum. Somehow we need to retain as much as possible for posterity, which means finding ways of preserving and updating traditional methods of farming without turning the countryside into an exhibit. Although it may involve some disappointments for the juggernauts of manufacturing industry, each innovation should be weighed most carefully against the old methods, and its consequences should be thoroughly investigated before it is introduced. At present, there is very little except the goodwill of the farmers to protect the fabric of the countryside: hedges can be ripped up, woodlands felled, meadows ploughed up and old farm buildings demolished with very little legal hindrance. The rights of farmers and visitors alike must be balanced by a greater awareness of their responsibilities. In the future, we will need the countryside more than ever.

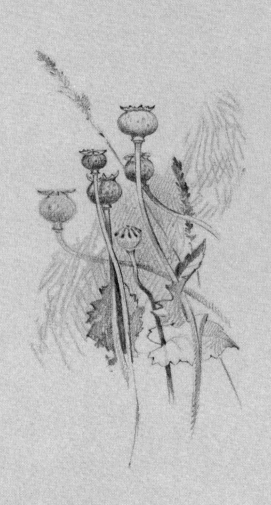

List of Pictures

The paintings and drawings that appear in this book were completed between January 1979 and May 1980 with the exception of the earlier oil paintings reproduced on pages 8–9, 67 and 84. These are included by kind permission of their owners.

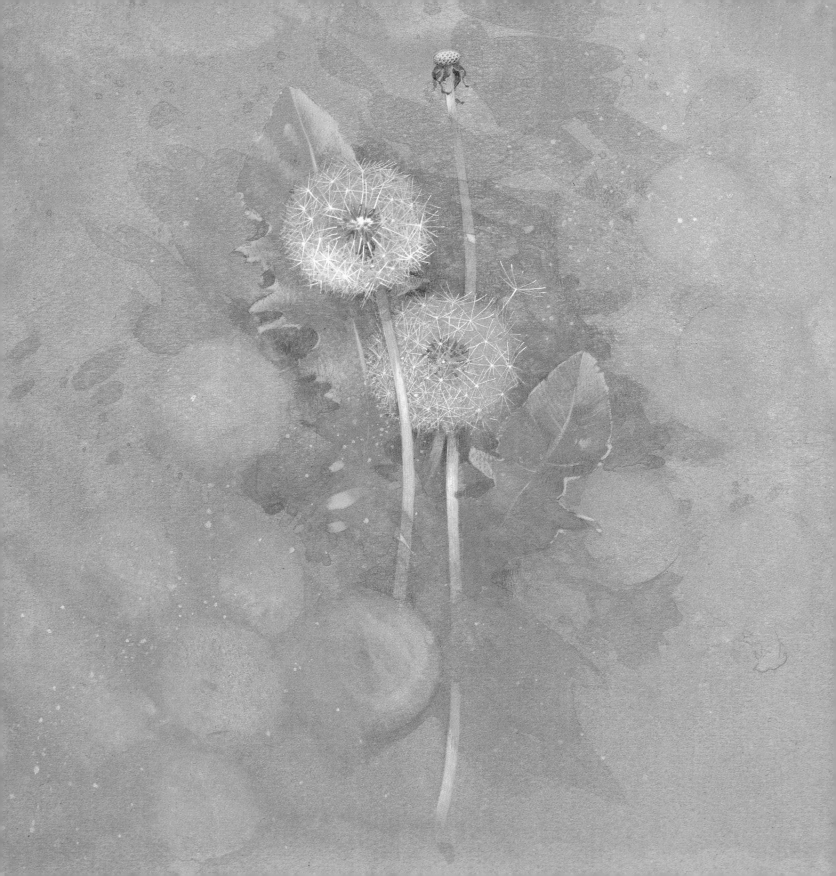